Unassuming Serial Killers

Nick Sutton

Published by Trellis Publishing, 2021.

UNASSUMING SERIAL KILLERS

NICK SUTTON

necessarily wish to have James in their lives, they felt that it was a better situation for him to be in than a foster home. They were well aware of the mental issues that he had been having. James would take on the last name of Wood from this point on.

As James grew older, his actions seemed to only cross the line farther and more often. When he was 14 years old, he stole his first car. While this could somewhat be classified as teenage stupidity in the rural lands of Idaho, his actions next would, again, cross the line. James took this car to several areas in the local town and set fire to each dumpster he came across. Eventually, he was arrested and returned home. Gene and Mildred Wood had been working hard to try and straighten James out. They had sent him off to St. Anthony's Youth Correction Center twice already to this point. They felt that this would not only help to control his behavior, but also allow him the opportunity to talk with people about some of the things he had seen throughout his miserable childhood. After this incident, they decided that something else had to be done.

In 1961, just before James Edward Wood turned 15, he was released by his family to the state of Idaho. He officially became a ward of the state. The reasoning behind this was quite simple. They had seen countless signs that he was mentally disturbed and violent. He was not at all close with them in the sense that he didn't want to speak with them and work with them. James was sent to reform school at this time. For all intents and purposes, he had reached the end of the line. Something had to give. For James Edward Wood, it wouldn't take long for his life to completely spiral out of control.

In 1964, James Edward Wood was released from reform school. He was 17 years old at this time. The school was left with little choice at this point with his age. He was released on a strict condition. James was told that he had to leave the state and return to live with his natural father, who was in Louisiana. Earnest had been out of prison for several years at this point but had little to no contact with James. James was aware that Earnest had a successful business selling and installing chain link fencing. James agreed to this request, however he would never make good on this promise.

It was at this time that James Edward Wood was first sent to prison. Still in his teenage years, he had been caught committing several small crimes in Idaho and Louisiana. He was convicted and given a minor sentence. James Wood, however, didn't care to follow through with an authority figure telling him what to do. He tried to escape an unbelievable 7 times.

In the same year, he successfully escaped prison one of these times. He famously acquired a knife from the mess hall at the jail. He was able to put one of the guards in a head lock. In this position, he threatened the life of the guard and the guard's family in an effort to coerce his way out of the cell. This plan worked. He had escaped jail, at least momentarily. He would quickly be caught and put back in jail to finish his sentence. In early 1966, he was released from prison. He had again been given another chance to prove that he could function in society.

In December of 1966, James Edward Wood would again find himself on the wrong side of the law. In a move that was highly publicized in his court proceedings some 25 years later, he killed a colt that was tied to a tree in Louisiana. James would say that he really had no good reason to kill the colt. He killed the colt, truly, just to be mean. It was such a cold blooded act for no apparent reason. As information would come out to police who were investigating the crime, the colt was a Christmas gift to a young woman in the area. Although never confirmed, it is suspected that James Wood knew the colt was a gift to this young woman and wanted to kill the horse to get at the girl.

For the next several years, James Wood was on the run for several petty crimes, including the killing of the colt. Ironically enough, in this time he was able to find some version of love. In 1967, at the ripe age of 20 years old, James Edward Wood married his first wife. Angie Bell was a seemingly normal woman. She took on a similar persona as Wood did, an unassuming young woman who came across as genuine, sincere, and simple. She knew very little about who James Wood really was. She failed to take note of the signs of his mental state. She would soon realize the man that James Edward Wood was shaping up to be.

The couple had a child within the first year of being married. Angie Bell would quickly divorce James when she learned of his sentence to prison for his seemingly countless petty crimes. This was not something that Angie wanted to be around. She would not be out of his life forever, though.

James Wood was sentenced to prison for a second time. He would now be serving his time at Angola State Penitentiary. Angola State was known as one of the dirtiest and harshest prison environments in the south during this period of time. It was Louisiana's major state penitentiary. James would be housed with some of the toughest criminals in the south. In 1967, he began his second term in jail.

In 1969, James Edward Wood committed his first official rape. He was still in jail at the time. James was very open to the fact that he had sexual desires for both men and women. He was adamant that this was his first rape that he had committed up until his death. James Edward Wood would serve four and a half years of his sentence. He was released in 1971. Yet again, James had a clean slate.

For the better half of the next decade, James Wood lived out a sad and unassuming existence in the public eye. To anyone around him, he seemed like a normal human. No one knew of his past convictions and his mental make-up. Only after his death would his actions in this period be truly understood.

In 1974, astonishingly, Angie remarried James. The couple had yet another child. Angie's family strongly disapproved and couldn't understand how she could go back to James. Angie would not stay with James long, as she would file for a final divorce just two months after giving birth to their second child.

In 1979, at the age of 32, James Edward Wood was sentenced to a major jail sentence. He was given 10 years for armed robbery and rape charges. It is suspected at this time that he committed as many as 30 robberies across 3 states. In addition to his robberies, it would later be proven as to how many murders and rapes he committed in this span as well. In any event, James Edward Wood was off the streets and back in Angola State Penitentiary.

James Wood would serve just six years of his ten year sentence. Shockingly, he was released on good behavior. More than likely, the truth behind his release was economically based. That has neither been proven nor disproven up to this point.

Upon his release from jail, James Edward Wood moved to Texas officially. He moved in with Earnest Arnold, his half-brother from his father's first marriage. It was at this time that Wood took a job as a truck driver for a carnival based out of Tyler, Texas. In this job, he was on the road for extended periods of time. The carnival would never stay in an area more than a week. It is widely believed based off of spotty testimony by Wood himself that he committed dozens of rapes and murders during this time. He was able to take advantage of the fact that he would never stay in a place long enough for people to recognize him.

In 1986, after living with his brother for just a few months, he was kicked out of the house. Earnest strongly disapproved of his relationship with a man named Jimmy Twiggs. Twiggs and Wood had met at their stay together at Angola. It was at this time they formed a sexual relationship that was now entering the home of Earnest Arnold. Wood agreed to leave the home.

In 1990, at age 43, Wood severely injured his left hand. He was using a power saw and got his hand caught in the blade. Three of his fingers were nearly cut off. Doctors saved his hand and his fingers by performing emergency surgery. His hand would always remain extremely weak. This is important to note, as Woods' lawyers tried to use this angle in aspects of his murder trial.

In 1992, James Wood decided to head back to Idaho being as he had no place to stay. On his way through Colorado, he robbed a Pizza Hut in Denver. On October 31, 1992, Wood arrived back in Pocatello, Idaho and moved in with his cousin Dave Haggard. While Haggard was hesitant to let James live with him, he agreed only until Wood could get back on his feet. James got a job at a local restaurant in Pocatello the following month. In his spare time, James Wood made eerie paintings on saw blades. Even with all of his mental health issues and criminal history, he was quite the artist.

It was in November of 1992 that the final fall for James Wood would begin. On November 28, 1992, just one month after arriving back in Idaho, Wood committed a rape. He stalked a 15 year old woman named Beth Edwards from her job at a Pizza Hut. As she was leaving to the parking lot, Wood abducted her and raped her.

Just two months later, he robbed a Subway at gunpoint in Pocatello. This was the initial crime in Idaho that got police tracking him. They suspected more was going on with Wood. They were aware of his past. The Subway robbery put him back on their radar.

In the spring of 1993, the 45 year old James Wood committed the next horrific crime. He had been casually dating a woman he had recently met. She had a young, 14 year old daughter named Karen. Wood raped Karen after her mother had left the house.

Less than one month later, Wood committed yet another high profile robber, this time of a Sizzler Steak house in Salt Lake City, Utah. Less than one hour later, he picked a woman up off of the street and raped her in his car before murdering her.

At this point, the police had enough evidence from his armed robberies to send Wood away to prison for likely his entire life. It is important to understand that his rape and murder crimes were not known to police.

On June 29, 1993, James Edward Wood committed one of the most high profile crimes of the 1990's. While he had committed numerous rapes, robberies, and murders to this point, most of them were not known until after his initial murder trial. It was the crime that he committed in on this day that would see that his terrible crime streak would end.

Jeralee Underwood was a 10 year old girl that lived in Woods' neighborhood in Pocatello, Idaho. She delivered the newspapers to the entire neighborhood each day. Wood observed her for several weeks. He knew her route and the stops she made. He knew what time she would be at certain locations. It was this sick and twisted planning that allowed him to take her without being seen.

James Wood abducted Jeralee Underwood as she was delivering papers. He quickly grabbed her and put her in his car. Initially, he didn't harm her. He drove her out to a secluded part of the woods. The area was vastly overgrown and not frequented often by anyone. He told Jeralee to get out to use the bathroom. As she exited the vehicle, James Wood shot her in the head. He then dismembered her body there in the woods. Little Jeralee Underwood was dead at just 10 years old at the hands of the monster of a man that was James Wood.

On July 6, 1993, Wood was arrested for the murder of Jeralee Underwood. After years of dodging the law and getting away with countless crimes, he had finally committed a crime that someone had witnessed and reported. Upon his arrest, Wood led police to the body of Underwood. He had taken the parts of her body and thrown them into Snake River.

Upon questioning James Wood, it was clear to investigators that this man had a story to tell that went well beyond Jeralee Underwood. While they suspected him of dozens of murders and rapes that had been unsolved in his locations over the years, they only gained one true murder confession from him beyond the Underwood case. He confessed to murdering a Louisiana woman all the way back in 1976. While this confession was not possible to convict and try him for, investigators felt like he was playing a sick mind game with them. In their minds, Wood wanted them to know that he had committed many other murders.

In a case that was as close to a sure conviction as can be found, the trial went largely without a hitch. Pocatello police detective Scott Shaw found himself in the national spotlight throughout the investigation, trial, and ultimate story of James Edward Wood. Shaw has discussed incredibly eerie viewpoints into the mind of James Wood. In an article for the *Associated Press* published on December 17, 1994, Shaw paints an incredibly real picture into the investigation and questioning of Wood.

As has been discussed, James Wood was quite an artist. After his arrest in July of 1993, Wood painted a self-portrait in his jail cell in Idaho. His intention was to gift this portrait to Shaw, the lead investigator who arrested him. The portrait itself is chilling. In the picture, a cross and scale of justice is seen above Woods' head. On his neck is a portrait of Jeralee Underwood. One the other side of his neck is a long line of altars that 'fade away into infinity.' Each platform has the body of woman across it.

"He told me, 'Those are the people I've killed,'" Shaw said.

This is completely disturbing on numerous levels. Perhaps the most unnerving aspect of this is that Wood drew this picture just weeks after committing his famous murder. To gift this to the investigator that arrested you is simply mind blowing.

The night of the arrest of James Wood was unique for the entire case and really shaped the personality of Wood. Shaw was the lead investigator that heard the hours of confession that Wood gave on that eerie night. The truth of who Wood really was would finally be known.

Wood not only confessed to the murder of Underwood, but also the murder of a pregnant mother in Louisiana. As was his typical style, he abducted her from a parking lot on Christmas Eve and raped her repeatedly. He eventually would go on to kill her and dismember her body. Police would find her skull in a heavily wooded area nearly 5 years later. By that time, there was no way for investigators in Louisiana to identify who committed the murder. Her case was cold until Wood confessed in Idaho on the fateful evening.

In addition to the two murder confessions, Wood also confessed to the brutal rapes and attempted murders of two other teenage women. One young woman was from Bridgeton, Missouri and the other was a local Pocatello teenager. Both women luckily survived. Jamie Masengil, the rape victim from Missouri, testified against Wood in court at his sentencing hearing.

To truly understand how calculated and evil James Edward Wood was, look no further than the events that surround the rape and attempted murder of Masengil.

"She survived by the Grace of God," Wood would later say.

On that fateful night in November of 1992, James Wood abducted and raped Jamie Masengil from a parking lot. His plan all along was to rape and murder the 15 year old teenage woman. After he had driven her to the outer reaches of town, he raped her. If this wasn't bad enough, Masengil's two-year-old baby sister was in the back seat of the vehicle as he raped her. After he finished committing this terrible act, he forced the teenager out of the car. She was told to kneel on the ground next to the vehicle.

"The snow was very deep," Wood proclaimed. "It was already going to be a tricky situation."

Jamie Masengil was on her knees in the deep snow just outside the car. Wood put the gun to the back of her head and pulled the trigger. To his surprise, the gun jammed. Like a true criminal who had much experience in committing these heinous acts, he knew that he had to act quickly. He knew there was neighbors just 100 feet away that would likely be startled by the gun shot. He also decided that if he unjammed the shell and shot his next round, that he would then have two shell casings to pick up rather than one. He concluded that in the deep snow it would take too long and prove too risky.

There is no sane way that a criminal thinks. Many criminals are caught before they even make one move to escape due to mistakes and evidence being left behind. Most criminals don't think like James Wood did. It was due to this gun jamming that spared the life of Jamie Masengil. He felt comfortable fleeing on foot. He knew he was unlikely to ever see this victim again. He also knew that he had gotten away with similar crimes numerous times before.

Many who dove deep into the life and crimes of James Wood feel strongly that he has committed an extraordinary amount of crimes. The common theme to his madness, especially in the 1980's and early 1990's, was to rape his victims in a secluded area before killing them. Many times, as he would later profess, he raped the victim's body after he had dealt the fatal blow. His portrait and his highly publicized confessions to Shaw also lead many to conclude that there were many murder victims that perhaps will never be discovered. Most estimates put this number at as many as 150 rape occurrences and over 50 murders. With his style of quickly leaving areas and moving across the country, many cases simply went cold. Most cases were discovered after he was well out of town. The true number of victims at the hands of James Wood will likely never be known.

The jury found James Wood guilty of several counts of rape and capital murder on January 1, 1994. With a quick deliberation, he was sentenced to death by way of lethal injection. As is common with murder cases, several appeals were filed by his team. After several rejections and even a stay of execution by Supreme Court Justice O'Connor in 1998, Wood would ultimately lose out. The Supreme Court refused to hear Wood's appeal in a final decision on May 16, 1999.

James Edward Wood would never face the justice that so many people deserved to see him serve. Instead of lethal injection, he died in his sleep of a heart attack on February 1, 2004. He was on death row at the time of his death. Many feel that while the justice system ultimately got the case correctly, it took too long and Wood should have been executed long before natural causes sealed his fate.

The legacy of James Wood is largely unknown. While he ultimately was convicted of the brutal rape and murder of an innocent 10-year-old girl in 1994, the true scope of his crimes will truthfully never be known. He was an unassuming man that lurked in the shadows, waiting for the opportunity to find his next victim. Circumstance played a key role in the man that he became. While a miserable childhood is certainly no excuse to commit such evil acts, it certainly helps others to comprehend how he could veer so far off the straight path at such an early age. James Wood was a rapist, a murderer, and a pedophile who never truly showed any remorse for the terrible things that he did. His legacy is best remembered as an evil human who took the lives and emotional sanity of so many people over a 20 year span.

TOY BOX KILLER

NATALIE MARSHALL

David Parker Ray was a suspected American serial killer and known torturer and serial rapist of women; suspected because no bodies were ever found. However, he was accused by his accomplices of murdering a number of women and law enforcement officials estimate that he is responsible for as many as 60 deaths in and near Truth or Consequences, New Mexico. Ray purchased and refitted a trailer into what he called his "toy box" which was replete with a number of sex toys and torture items for his victims. He also played a very disturbing audiotape for all of his victims explaining what they will be enduring at his hand. Ray was finally arrested after one of his victims managed to escape after three days of torture. Ray stood trial for kidnapping and sexual torture and was sentenced to 224 years in prison; however, he suffered a fatal heart attack while incarcerated at Lea County Correctional Facility in Hobbs, New Mexico, on 28 May 2002.

Early Life

David Parker Ray was born on 6 November 1939, in Belen, New Mexico. He was named David after his uncle David who was accidentally shot in the heart at the age of 13 by his 15-year-old brother Alden just one year earlier. Ray's grandmother believed him to be a reincarnation of her dead son.

Ray's father, Cecil, was an alcoholic and was very abusive to both Ray and his sister Peggy—who was one year his junior—as well as their mother, Nettie. When Ray was ten years old his father left his mother and moved to Albuquerque. They were divorced soon thereafter. When Nettie decided to stay with her own parents, Ray and Peggy were shipped off to their paternal grandparents, Ethan and Dolly Ray. In the six years Ray and Peggy lived with their grandparents they saw their father twice and their mother only a handful of times. Consequently, there were no maternal bonds between Nettie and her children. In fact, Ray said that he didn't get much affection or attention at all during his childhood.

Ethan was a strict disciplinarian who insisted on the utmost standards of dress and behavior and, as such, the children were required to do ranch chores both before and after school and even though the Rays were not very well off, Ethan made sure his grandchildren were clean and presentable. He was also a devout fundamentalist Christian and made sure to instill within his grandchildren his religious beliefs. Any nonadherence to his rules resulted in physical punishment.

Ray attended Mountainair High School in Mountainair, New Mexico, where he was often bullied for his awkwardness and shyness, especially around girls. Ray commented that he didn't have his first date until he was 18 years old. He was also tormented for being soft-spoken and for having to keep his shirt buttoned all the way to the top—per his grandfather's instructions—when all of the other boys had a few top buttons undone. Ray was also a poor student.

Neighbor Audie Miranda always tried to look out for Ray. He would tell the bullies to leave him alone and stated that even though Ray could defend himself, he remained docile, not liking or believing in violence which was ironic considering what Ray would become. The two became close friends and spent a lot of time together on the Ray ranch riding horses, playing cowboys and Indians, and playing desert hide-and-seek.

Ray always had a love of the outdoors.

Miranda would later say that he believed that Ray's ultra-strict upbringing took a toll on his friend. Miranda even commented that he, himself, was scared of Ethan.

Dolly was not much better. Ray said that he hated her and that she "didn't have a clue."

At the age of 12, Ray began building and setting off bombs and other explosives he fashioned in the woods behind his grandparents' house. He said he blew up a lot of tree stumps as a child.

When Ray was 13 his grandparents gave him a Cushman Pacemaker motor scooter. He discovered within himself a natural aptitude for mechanics and delighted in taking it apart and then reassembling it. The once shy and timid Ray became more confident, especially when his classmates who used to torment him needed his services to fix their scooters.

Some accounts state that Ray began to use and abuse alcohol and drugs while in high school. It was also around this time he began to fantasize about raping, torturing, and murdering women. He said that the few times his father would come visit them, he would bring true detective magazines which Ray enjoyed reading. He began having his fantasies which always involved broken bottles. His sister stumbled upon Ray's sadomasochistic drawings as well as erotic photographs of acts of bondage.

At the age of 15 Ray fashioned his own little dungeon under a large piñon pine tree with a hangman's noose and a collection of broken beer bottles he "planned to use on girls someday." He also admitted to digging a hole and engaging in intercourse with the ground when he was lonesome.

After high school, Ray worked as an auto mechanic.

He married in 1959, joking that he was practically a virgin at that time, and joined the United States Army a year later where he was sent to Korea. The Rays had a son in 1960 and Ray had to return home on emergency leave because his wife was leaving the baby alone when she went out to party. He filed for divorce and sought sole custody. His mother, Opel, and stepfather, Cecil, raised Ray's son until Ray was honorably discharged from the military.

Ray married a second time in 1962 when he was 22 years old and a mere 90 days later he went back to court and filed for divorce again because they just didn't "click".

In 1966, Ray married a third time; to a woman named Glenda Burdine. They were married 15 years and had a daughter named Glenda Jean—who would go by "Jesse"—in 1969. Jesse remembered her father as being gone quite a bit, having worked for the railroad, and of having an unusual fetish for padded leather straps and other bondage fare. She said that kids were naturally curious and while they knew about it, it was not a topic to be discussed.

In sum, Ray married four times, was divorced four times, and had two children.

Ray met Cindy Lea Hendy in 1997 when he was 57; she was 20 years his junior. Originally from Washington, Hendy and her boyfriend John Youngblood moved to Truth or Consequences, New Mexico, on the run from the law for grand theft, forgery, and drug offenses, leaving her three children behind. As she had already served time in jail, she was not keen on returning.

The Crimes

The "Toy Box"

Ray spent over $100,000 on his homemade torture chamber he called his "toy box" that he constructed inside of an old white 15-feet-by-25-feet cargo trailer on his Elephant Butte, New Mexico, property. Elephant Butte is a resort town of approximately 2,000 residents, located along an 18-mile-long, 36,000-acre reservoir.

The trailer was stocked with what he referred to as his "friends": bully whips, pulleys, leather straps, metal clamps, bars which spread the victim's legs, surgical knifes and saws which he used to torture women. Inside this trailer were also numerous sex toys, syringes, detailed diagrams that showed different methods for inflicting pain and torture, and a homemade electrical generator. Ray also mounted a mirror on the ceiling above the gynecologist table upon which he strapped his victims because he wanted them to see everything that was done to them.

He also played a recorded audiotape of himself for his victims whenever they regained consciousness. It began with:

*"Hello there, b*tch. Are you comfortable right now? I doubt it. Wrists and ankles chained. Gagged. Probably blind folded. You are disoriented*

*and scared, too, I would imagine. Perfectly normal, under the circumstances. For a little while, at least, you need to get your sh*t together and listen to this tape. It is very relevant to your situation. I'm going to tell you, in detail, why you have been kidnapped, what's going to happen to you and how long you'll be here. I don't know the details of your capture, because this tape is being created July 23rd, 1993, as a general advisory tape for future female captives. The information I'm going to give you is based on my experience dealing with captives over a period of several years. If, at a future date, there are any major changes in our procedures, the tape will be upgraded. Now, you are obviously here against your will, totally helpless, don't know where you're at, don't know what's gonna happen to you. You're very scared or very pissed off. I'm sure that you've already tried to get your wrists and ankles loose, and know you can't. Now you're just waiting to see what's gonna happen next."*

The rest of the tape involves Ray setting forth his "rules" and "procedures" by telling his victims everything—in graphic detail—that would be done to them to include being raped and sodomized by Ray and his friends, engaging in bestiality, being shocked with electricity, and being poked and prodded with a multitude of surgical instruments and sex toys; essentially, being their sex slave to do with whatever they want. The actual recording is widely available online, quite long, and not for the faint of heart as it is extremely explicit.

In the audiotape Ray describes himself as a "dungeon master" who was affiliated with the Church of Satan and that his slaves were for members of his "congregation."

There was also a videotape showing Ray and his girlfriend Cindy Lea Hendy performing such acts of torture upon a female victim who screamed the entire time.

Psychological torture was also important to Ray. He would blindfold his victims, subject them to brainwashing, use fear tactics, and occasional small favors to keep them "off balance".

Many experts classify Ray as a sexual sadist who finds excitement and pleasure from inflicting pain upon a nonconsensual, submissive and inducing them into altered states of consciousness such as when they pass out from the pain. Such a predilection often forms during adolescence; however, experts do not know exactly what causes one to become a sexual sadist.

Ray had multiple accomplices during this time; including, allegedly, several of his girlfriends, particularly his latest girlfriend, Hendy.

During the investigation Hendy allegedly had told a friend—while she was under the influence of alcohol—that she had willingly participated in Ray's attacks because of the adrenaline rush she got from them. She allegedly confided to this person that "there were four to six people who had been killed, dismembered, and tossed into Elephant Butte Lake." While the friend did not initially believe her, after Ray and Hendy were arrested and the details of the crimes were released, he gave statements to police and the media.

Marie Parker

On 5 July 1997, 22-year-old Marie Parker and her two daughters—ages four and five—were evicted from their apartment for non-payment of rent. They were living in a pup tent on the western shore of Elephant Butte Lake at a campsite called Hot Springs Cove; just north of Ray's trailer. In fact, she had borrowed the tent from him and when her campsite became too messy for the fastidious Ray, he had something to say about it.

Parker was a methamphetamine and cocaine junkie and her main supplier was Ray's daughter Jesse. Ray abducted Parker and took her to his toy box where he raped and tortured her for three days after which he gave Yancy a rope and told him that they "were finished" with her. He then told Yancy to kill her which Yancy admitted to doing. They buried the body in a remote area and Ray threatened Yancy's life if he ever told anyone.

Later, when police took Yancy to the area where Parker's body was allegedly dumped, they could not find any evidence. Yancy stated that Ray probably moved the body.

Police found Parker's abandoned car in the parking lot of the Blue Waters Saloon.

Cynthia Vigil

Cynthia Vigil had been working as a prostitute along Central Avenue (Highway 66) at around 10:00 a.m. when her pimp introduced her to Ray and Hendy in a red recreational vehicle. Ray offered Vigil $20 for oral sex and when she entered the vehicle, Ray produced a police badge and told Vigil that she was under arrest for solicitation. Ray and Hendy handcuffed, gagged, and chained Vigil to a fixture inside of the camper. After a few minutes he pulled the vehicle over and then proceeded to cut off all of her clothing, put a metal dog collar around her neck, place her in shackles, and then slipped a leather mask over her head with no eye openings and a zipper for the mouth. She was also told if she resisted she would be shocked.

When they reached Ray's house, after driving for an hour, Vigil said that she was chained to a bed and was made to listen to Ray's infamous five-minute audiotape before being forced to have sex with both Ray and Hendy. Next, Vigil said that Ray put gravy "up" her and had his German shepherd lick it off. Vigil then had her knees attached to a bar, forcing her legs open and was then "measured" with dildoes that had markings on them before having her breasts and genitals shocked with a portable generator. The entire time Hendy had a gun pointed at her.

The next morning, Vigil was taken at gunpoint to the bathroom to relieve herself and then taken back to the bed, fresh and clean white sheets atop it, where her mouth and eyes were duct taped and she was hog-tied with an elaborate collection of interconnected leather straps. A rope was then attached to a pulley from the ceiling and Vigil's entire body was lifted three feet into the air.

The duct tape was ripped from her eyes and she saw her horrified face staring back at her from a video monitor. She said that Ray tied her legs open and proceeded to whip her with a leather belt, whips, and a cat-o' nine tails. Vigil said that the beating excited Ray who then violated her with a "horrendous looking dildo" and took pictures of her suspended body with the toys inside of her.

Later that day he attached an elaborate system of clamps and pulleys to her breasts and genitalia and proceeded to shock her. Her convulsions caused the pulleys to exert force on the clamps. After taking the excruciating pain for as long as she could, she lost consciousness.

For the next two days Vigil was subjected to sexual torture until she was able to escape.

On 22 March 1999, Cynthia Vigil escaped after being abducted by Ray and enduring a three-day torture ordeal. She was able to escape one morning after Ray had left for work and Hendy had left the keys on a nearby table when the latter went into another room to talk on the phone. Vigil—chained to the wall in the den—managed to use her legs and feet to pull the table toward her and get the keys; however, Hendy noticed her efforts and a fight ensued. Vigil was able to free herself while Hendy beat her and even after being hit in the head with a lamp, Vigil managed to stab Hendy in the back of the neck with an icepick she found on the floor. When Hendy fell to the ground, Vigil escaped the house naked save for an iron slave collar and padlocked chains, and began to run down Bass Road in Elephant Butte. Since she had just been taken three days ago, Vigil had not been taken out to the toy box yet.

Vigil was spotted by a couple of passing motorists who did not know what to make of the woman and didn't stop. Vigil finally surprised a woman at home in her trailer watching television who called the police for her. Vigil was then taken to the Sierra Vista

County Hospital emergency room where the chains were cut off and her battered body was cared for.

When police went to Ray's home, they found bloodied sheets in one bedroom with a broken lamp and broken window, thus corroborating Vigil's claims. A pulley device with hooks and chains was mounted on the ceiling and there was a long, coffin-like box along the side of the bed. Large sex toys were on the dresser.

Arrest and Investigation

After Vigil's escape, Ray and Hendy were arrested off Springfield Road in his red Toyota camper. They claimed that they had kidnapped Vigil in an effort to break her of her heroin addiction. Ray and Hendy were taken to nearby Truth or Consequences—formerly Hot Springs—New Mexico and housed in the Cooper Police Training Center.

Both Ray and Hendy were charged with 12 counts consisting of aggravated kidnapping, conspiracy, and aggravated battery and held on $1 million bail.

Soon after Ray was arrested, New Mexico State Police took the case over from the Truth or Consequences Police Department and Agent Wesley LaCuesta—a five-year veteran of the Criminal Assault and Violent Crimes Division—was called on to assist in the investigation. He left his Las Cruces office and headed north to Truth or Consequences.

LaCuesta interviewed Vigil at the hospital. He observed many small cuts on her extremities, injuries to her breasts, welts on her back, and evidence of her being handcuffed.

By early April 1999, over 100 New Mexico State Police and FBI agents were all over Ray's property looking for human remains.

Eleven days after his arrest, Patty Rust committed suicide after assisting law enforcement personnel with detailed drawings of the toy box over the course of four days. Prosecutor Jim Yontz wondered why the FBI would send a woman into a torture chamber where many women had likely been frightened to death by Ray and the torture he inflicted upon them. He then went to visit the toy box. Inside he found a ghastly collection of sex toys, medical devices, whips, clamps, chains, pulleys, rods, saws, and other items for bondage and sadomasochism; in addition to detailed drawings of how Ray liked to torture his victims, medical books on the female anatomy, and, perhaps most damning, a videotape dating back to 1993 showing a woman being tortured.

There was also a television monitor in the right corner of the toy box so Ray's victims could see what he was doing to them if they looked at the monitor while they were secured to the table. He also had a video camera focused upon the table recording everything he was doing. Photographs of the torture he had inflicted upon prior victims decorated the walls, as well as a bunch of dolls which were "strung up in various states of bondage and torture." In addition to the medical texts, Ray had a copy of Brett Easton Ellis' *American Psycho*; a novel detailing violent assaults inflicted by a man when he needed to release steam from his high-stress life that was also made into a film starring Christian Bale. The novel contains very disturbing descriptions of torture. It was presumed that Ray compared himself to the "protagonist" in the novel as he saw himself as in control and his victims as "expendable pawns in his game", even going so far as to call his victims "packages."

With respect to the videotape depicting the torture of one of Ray's victims, the police were able to find the woman on the tape: Kelly Garrett, who had been married mere days before being abducted by Ray and Hendy. Garrett had been held hostage, raped, and tortured for three days before being drugged and left on the side of the road not far from her in-laws' house. Believing Garrett had been out on a drug binge, she was asked to leave and subsequently moved back to Colorado. Investigators found her in Colorado and she stated that she had amnesia for a long time, only recently—as in the past year—remembering what Ray and Hendy had done to her.

The publicity surrounding the case prompted another victim to come forward with her story. Angelica Montano recounted her ordeal at Ray's hands just one month ago.

Angelica Montano

Montano said that she was a casual acquaintance of both Ray and Hendy and had gone to their house on 17 February 1999, looking to borrow cake mix. She said that Ray left the room and then returned with a knife and told her that she was being kidnapped. When Montano looked over at Hendy, she saw the woman holding a gun, pointed at her. She knew they were serious.

Montano said that the couple grabbed, bound, and stripped her before strapping her to a bed and placing a metal collar on her. She said they then attached electrodes to her breasts and shocked her multiple times in addition to "abus[ing] her with various sexual implements." She then said that Ray forced her to give him oral sex.

After having been chained naked to the bed for three days and being subjected to sexual abuse, it was time for Montano to visit the toy box. Ray removed her handcuffs and led her to the bathroom with a long metal leash attached to the dog collar. He bathed her "like a dog, with a chain and everything" Montano would later say. When she was clean, Hendy applied makeup to her face and then draped a robe over her captive's shoulders before Ray and Hendy led her out into the trailer.

In the smaller trailer—the toy box—Montano was strapped to a gynecologist table where she was subjected to additional electric shocks to her genitalia as well as other instances of sexual assault. She said that she repeatedly begged Ray and Hendy to release her and on the fourth day they relented. She was drugged and taken miles away from Ray's property and dumped on a local highway in the desert where a police officer found her.

Even though Montano did, in fact, report the incident to the police, there had been no follow up. When she saw that Ray and Hendy had been arrested, Montano contacted the police again.

Accomplices

In addition to Hendy, investigators discovered two other accomplices: Ray's daughter Glenda Jean "Jesse" Ray; and Dennis Roy Yancy. Yancy and Hendy had dated in the past.

Yancy admitted to strangling Marie Parker—a former girlfriend—after Ray kidnapped and tortured her. Ray videotaped the murder. Yancy also confessed to seeing photographs of one of Ray's ex-wives in various bondage positions as well as watching Ray torture a woman inside the toy box but that he thought it was consensual. Yancy was subsequently convicted of second-degree murder and conspiracy to commit first-degree murder. He received two 15-year sentences. Jesse was also tried and convicted of kidnapping for sexual torture. She was sentenced to seven years and served three, the rest of the time she was on parole.

Hendy was charged with 25 felonies and was looking at 197 years in prison. To save herself, she agreed to plead no contest and testify against Ray and Yancy in exchange for five felony counts and a 36-year sentence. In the Seventh District Court of New Mexico Hendy pled guilty to two counts of first-degree kidnapping for Vigil and Montano, two counts of sexual penetration (rape) in the second degree for the two women, and one count of conspiracy to commit second-degree kidnapping.

Over 100 FBI agents were sent to search Ray's property but they were unable to identify any human remains. Several bones were located but they proved to be of animal origin. Collecting evidence from Ray's home and toy box proved daunting due to the sheer number of items he had amassed for his tortuous pleasure. In one interview, New Mexico Public Safety Director Darren White told reporters that the evidence inside the toy box was "very disturbing stuff" and "literally made my stomach turn."

It was later discovered that Ray would drug his victims with sodium pentothal and phenobarbital to induce amnesia to prevent them from being able to report what had happened to them when they were released. In Kelly Garrett's case, she was unsure about her own recollections of the torture and accompanying nightmares; that is, until the FBI contacted her and, soon thereafter, she was able to remember—in vivid detail—what Ray did to her so she could testify against him in court.

In his recording, Ray described his whole philosophy about drugging his victims and why getting an accurate body count of those victims he killed is impossible. Ray said:

*"If I killed every b*tch that we kidnapped, there'd be bodies strung all over the country. And besides, I don't like killin' a girl, unless it is absolutely necessary. So I've devised a safe, alternate method of disposal. I had plenty of b*tches to practice on over the years, so I've pretty well got it down pat. And I enjoy doin' it. I get off on mind games. After we get completely through with you, you're gonna be drugged up real heavy, with a combination of Sodium Pentothal and Phenobarbital. They are both hypnotic drugs that will make you extremely susceptible to hypnosis, autohypnosis and hypnotic suggestion. You're gonna be kept drugged a couple of days, while I play with your mind. By the time I get through brainwashing you, you're not gonna remember a fu*kin' thing about this little adventure. You won't remember this place, us, or what has happened to you. There won't be any DNA evidence, because you'll be bathed, and both holes between your legs will be thoroughly flushed out. You'll be dressed, sedated, and turned loose on some country road, bruised, heh, sore all over, but nothing that won't heal up in a week or two. The thought of being brainwashed may not be appealing to you, but we been doin' it a long time and it works. And it's the lesser of two evils. I'm sure that you would prefer that, in lieu of being strangled or having your throat cut."*

One can only imagine the pure horror coursing through his victims' minds as they lay, chained atop his torture table, hearing—in very graphic detail—about what they will be enduring.

Trials and Convictions

The press jumped all over the case and soon discovered that everyone who seemingly knew Ray said that he seemed like a "regular" guy. He did not have any criminal record, nor were there any reports about potentially suspicious activities on his property which he leased from the park service. However, reports from the police indicated that he was considerably worse and darker than he initially seemed.

State District Judge Neil Mertz decided that Ray would undergo three separate trials: for Cynthia Vigil, for Angelica Montano, and for Kelly Garrett. The Vigil trial was set to start on 28 March 2000, in Tierra Amarilla. Judge Mertz suppressed Ray's early interviews with the New Mexico State Police and FBI and also banned the media from the voir dire. Just after jury selection, Ray allegedly suffered a heart attack and was taken to a hospital in Las Cruces. The judge postponed the trial for another week and then there were additional delays and several FBI expert witnesses were excluded.

Then, unexpectedly, Judge Mertz decided to start Garrett's trial for her 1996 kidnapping and torture even though it was the weakest case, evidence-wise. Nevertheless, Judge Mertz scheduled it for the end of May. Of course, Ray was pleased with the delays, not to mention Judge Mertz's exclusion of Ray's printed sheet of procedures for handling his slaves as well as all devices found in the trailer for Garrett's trial since nobody could prove they were there in 1996. This left the prosecution with the videotape and the victim's testimony.

When Vigil's trial was actually conducted, it ended in a mistrial because some jurors were not convinced that the women were completely held against their will and there was a subsequent retrial that resulted in convictions for all 12 counts with which Ray was charged.

Montano's trial was delayed indefinitely because, unfortunately, she was rushed to an Albuquerque hospital on 7 May 2001 with pneumonia where she died an hour later from heart failure. She was only 28 years old. As she was one of only three living, known witnesses who were going to testify against Ray, Montano's death dealt a huge blow to the prosecution. However, prosecutor Jim Yontz was prepared to try Ray for Montano's kidnapping and torture by utilizing videotaped statements she had made at a preliminary hearing on 15 and 16 April 1999.

When prosecutors started "closing in" on his daughter Jesse who assisted with some of Ray's earlier kidnappings, Ray decided to take a plea bargain. He received a sentence of 224 years in prison.

Ray suffered a fatal heart attack while incarcerated at Lea County Correctional Facility in Hobbs, New Mexico, on 28 May 2002.

Aftermath

Yancy was paroled in 2010 after serving 11 years of his sentence; however, his release was delayed because of difficulties stemming from his parole plan which had to be established before release. Three months after he was released in 2011, he was charged with violating his parole and subsequently returned to prison and required to serve his entire sentence until 2021.

Ray is suspected of murdering his one-time business partner, Billy Bowers. The two men bought, restored, and sold cars. On 22 September 1988, Bowers disappeared and his family immediately offered a $5,000 reward for any information leading to his safe return. On 28 September 1989, a fisherman found a male body floating in McCrea Canyon which is along the eastern shore of Elephant Butte Lake. The body was wrapped in a blue tarp and secured to two heavy boat anchors. It had a single bullet hole to the head and $49.47 in a pocket but no identification. There were no missing persons reports for a five-foot-ten-inch male in his late-30's or early-40's so the John Doe remained unidentified for over a decade until Cindy Hendy told police that Ray had murdered Bowers. Hendy admitted that Ray confessed the murder to her and told her that since then he had learned to open the victims' stomachs so they would "stay down" when submerged in water and not float to the surface as was the case with Bowers.

When the body was exhumed and dental records compared, the John Doe was, in fact, Bowers. His son Michael was able to retrieve the body of his long-lost father for a proper burial and some closure.

In November 2002, state police officially opened the toy box to the public in the hopes that renewed media attention might help identify additional victims. Inside were signs that said "Satan's Den" and "Bondage Room." The obstetrical table was still there with all of its clamps, leg stretchers, electric wires, chains, and straps. A steel cabinet held numerous surgical instruments and the coffin-shaped box used to terrorize and contain victims was nearby. Ray's meticulous records detailing what he did to his victims was also available. To ensure that none of his victims escaped, Ray had devised an elaborate alarm system and had written instructions to ensure that all straps were secure prior to leaving the toy box.

However, with Ray dead, the investigation went cold, especially since no bodies were ever found, no possible victims were identified, and no suspicious deaths which might have been loosely linked to Ray were solved. Despite the lack of any dead bodies, he is oft-labeled in numerous sources of literature as a serial killer.

According to Jim Fielder in his 2003 book *Slow Death*, both Vigil and Garrett went on to form relationships and start families of their own.

As recently as 2012, additional evidence has been uncovered which indicated there may be additional victims.

GRANNY KILLER

NATALIE MARSHALL

John Wayne Glover ("The Granny Killer")

John Wayne Glover—also known as the "Granny Killer"—was a serial killer who was active in Sydney, Australia, between 1989 and 1990 who murdered at least six—and as many as 13—elderly females after hitting them with a claw hammer and then ritually strangling them with their own pantyhose. It was widely believed that Glover's victims represented his mother and mother-in-law who he blamed for his misdeeds. He was ultimately sentenced to six life sentences without any possibility of release. Glover committed suicide by hanging himself on 9 September 2005.

Glover's importance in Australian history was that he was the first modern serial killer in Sydney and despite police ultimately catching him, one woman would lose her life as police waited outside of her door while surveilling their prime suspect.

Early Life

John Wayne Glover was born on 26 November 1932 in Wolverhampton, England. He was convicted of numerous petty crimes starting in 1947 for such insignificant crimes as stealing clothing and handbags.

Glover had always had troubled relationships with older women; particularly his mother, Freda, and, later, his mother-in-law. Freda had a number of husbands and several boyfriends and he always harbored resentment toward his mother for leaving his father. When his mother died, Glover's "bizarre fascination with older women increased" as he was no longer satisfied by simply looking at them; he had an overwhelming urge to touch them. He was simultaneously fascinated and repulsed by nursing homes. When his mother-in-law was placed into such a home, he began to look forward to visiting her on Sunday afternoons because he now had a legitimate excuse to be in a nursing home. He often roamed around, looking for the oldest and most frail woman he could find and, whenever possible, he would indecently touch them. Their distress added to his excitement. This excitement of his was a symptom of gerontophilia; a sexual preference for the elderly and the opposite of pedophilia. Both were sexual paraphilias—abnormal and often extreme sexual desires.

In 1956, Glover relocated to Australia where he first resided in Melbourne and, in 1968, he settled in Mosman, Sydney. Shortly after moving to Australia he was convicted on two counts of larceny in Victoria, as well as another theft charge in New South Wales. In 1962, he was also convicted on two counts of assaulting women in Melbourne, two counts of indecent assault, four other counts of larceny, and another assault with bodily harm. Surprisingly he only received three years' probation for his offenses.

The attacks were reportedly quite severe and on each occasion the victim had certain articles of clothing removed. Victims were wrestled to the ground while Glover violently tore off their clothing. One victim was a 25-year-old woman who was on her way home one night at approximately 10:30 p.m. when she was followed and subsequently chased down a dark suburban street. She was knocked to the ground unconscious and later awakened in a garden bleeding profusely. Her undergarments were in "a state of disarray". Her assailant had run away when she had screamed and, thus, alerted residents in the area.

At the time of this attack, the 29-year-old Glover was employed for the Australian Broadcasting Company as a rigger while living in Camberwell, Melbourne.

In 1965, however, retribution finally caught up with Glover when he was convicted of being a Peeping Tom and was sentenced to three months in prison. He only served six weeks.

In 1968, Glover married the well-to-do middle-class Jacqueline Gail ("Gay") Rolls who he had met when he was working at a wine and spirits store in Melbourne. She fell in love with him despite his being from a very poor working-class family and having arrived in Australia with only $3 (30 shillings) to his name. Gay's father, John Rolls, believed that the quiet, handsome young man was a good match for his beloved daughter. Whereas her mother thought the same in the beginning, she later decided that her future son-in-law had something to hide. Nevertheless, they gave the couple their blessings and Gay and Glover married soon thereafter and moved into her parents' comfortable house. The Glovers had two daughters: Kellie who was born in 1971; and Marney who came along in 1973. Later, a separate wing was added to the Rolls' house so the young family could have some privacy away from Essie's tyrannical nature.

In 1982, Glover's oft-married mother—now known as Freda Underwood—showed up on his doorstep. He loathed her almost as much as he despised his mother-in-law. His mother eventually died of breast cancer in 1988 in Gosford, 100 kilometers north of Sydney where Glover convinced her to move. After being diagnosed with the same cancer—which is rare in men—Glover underwent a mastectomy and then developed a prostate condition that rendered him sexually impotent.

Before he began killing in the late 1980s he had volunteered at the Senior Citizens Society and was considered among those who knew him as a trustworthy and friendly bloke.

Glover's family had no clue that he was the serial killer for whom the entire nation was looking. At this time he worked as a sales representative for Four 'n' Twenty Pies.

Prior to 1989, at the age of 56, when he allegedly started his murder spree (because there is some evidence that he may have been responsible for other murders committed prior to then), there was no proof that Glover had killed anyone up to that point. He had been married for 20 years when he started killing and in addition to having no clue about his predilections and murderous activities, his wife also had no knowledge of his previous convictions.

After each murder, Glover callously went about his life as normal.

The Crimes

Margaret Todhunter, 84

Before he began to kill, Glover had a "pre-murder" offense. On 11 January 1989, Glover witnessed 84-year-old Margaret Todhunter walking down Hale Road in Mosman. After he parked his vehicle he walked over to Todhunter, punched her in the face, and then stole the contents of her purse which included $209 that he spent at the Mosman RSL club, also called the Mosman Returned Servicemen's Club, on Military Road.

Investigators attributed the incident to a mugging and had little hope of finding out who the assailant was. Thankfully, she survived and only required eight stitches to close her head wound. Her description of her assailant would later prove pivotal in identifying Glover.

Gwendoline Mitchelhill, 82

On 1 March 1989, Glover was leaving the Mosman RSL when he saw 82-year-old Gwendoline Mitchelhill walking down the street toward her home in the upper middle-class suburb of Mosman. She lived in Camelia Gardens, an apartment block on Military Road where most of the residents were elderly widows even though there were also families and children.

Glover went to his car—a blue Falcon—removed a hammer, and hid it under his belt. He then followed Mitchelhill her entry door and as she opened it, he hit her on the back of her head with the hammer. He then continued to hit her with the hammer and his fists in her head and body, breaking several of her ribs.

Glover took Mitchelhill's purse which contained $100 and fled.

Two schoolboys exiting the elevator on the ground floor saw the victim attempting to crawl to the glass security doors at the front of the building with blood dripping from the serious wounds across her head. Her stockings had been torn from her legs and her cane and purse were laying further away. Her purse showed signs that someone had riffled through it. Other bystanders who came around to see what had happened, believing she had fallen and hit her head and, thus, paid no mind to the neat arrangement of her personal items. The boys quickly sought help.

There were no eyewitnesses to the actual attack or any clues or leads, nor was there any evidence to link this attack with Todhunter's earlier one. Compounding the problem was that good-hearted neighbors thought that Mitchelhill had simply fallen and, consequently, washed the crime scene of blood and any potential forensic evidence.

Police—not unlike Todhunter's assault—chalked this attack up as a mugging gone wrong.

Mitchelhill was rushed to the emergency room by ambulance and doctors worked quickly in an attempt to prevent further blood accumulation in her brain. During their examinations they decided that she simply had not fallen because her wounds were inconsistent with a fall. Instead, they determined that her head injuries, broken ribs, and dual black eyes suggested assault and contacted the Mosman police. Additionally, one of the ambulance medics told police of his concern regarding her purse that had been looked through but then placed neatly with the rest of her belongings. Later examination found that her wallet was not in her purse even though she did, in fact, have it earlier that day.

Unfortunately, Mitchelhill died that same evening.

A post-mortem examination the next day revealed "severe bruising to the right eye consistent with a fist, severe bruising to the right shoulder consistent with a blunt object, two wounds to back of the skull consistent with a blunt object, seven broken ribs consistent with a fist". The cause of death was attributed to her head and chest injuries which were determined to be consistent with a vicious attack. There was no evidence of sexual assault or other tampering.

Lady Winfreda Ashton, 84

On 9 May, Glover saw 84-year-old Lady Winfreda Ashton—the widow of renowned landscape painter Sir William Ashton—walking toward him on Military Road, on her way home to her Raglan Street residence. She kept her appointment at the Sydney eye hospital before going to the Mosman RSL until 2:30 p.m. She then stopped in to her local bank before proceeding to the nearby supermarket where she stopped to visit with friends. On her way home, she paused at her mailbox before heading toward the front entrance lobby of the building in which her unit was located.

Glover, donning a pair of gloves, followed her into her foyer where he attacked her with his hammer before throwing her to the ground and then dragging her into a trash bin alcove where he repeatedly bashed her head on the pavement. Glover later recalled that she had almost overpowered him, causing him to fall atop her, when he decided to hit her head on the pavement. Once she was unconscious, Glover removed her pantyhose and strangled her with them.

He then placed her shoes and cane by her feet and left with her purse which contained $100. Glover again went to the Mosman RSL where he commented to staff there that he "hoped that the sirens outside weren't for another mugging".

A neighbor found Ashton lying face-down diagonally across the concrete floor of the rubbish bin alcove with a pool of blood around her head. Her pantyhose were pulled so tightly around her neck that they had cut through her skin. She had a thin trickle of blood running from her mouth, her bare legs were crossed, and her arms were placed by her sides. Her cane and shoes were near her body and her purse had been opened, her wallet missing.

Detective Senior Constable Paul Mayger commented to his partner Detective Senior Constable Murray Byrnes that her murder had to have been committed by the same person who had already murdered once already and likely had assaulted another elderly woman.

At this point police believed that they may have a serial killer on the loose as all three victims thus far were wealthy elderly women who lived in the same area and were all assaulted or killed in the same manner before their purses were stolen. Ashton's injuries paralleled Mitchelhill's. The two crime scenes were only approximately one kilometer apart and both murder victims were killed at the entrance to their residences.

Ashton's autopsy was conducted by Argentinian-born Dr. Liliana Schwartz and this was her first homicide as a forensic pathologist in Australia. Schwartz checked the victim's body temperature, the extent of rigor mortis, and whether there were any signs of sexual assault; the latter which she determined did not occur as there was no evidence of semen. The ligature mark around her neck measured nine centimeters and she had bruising on her nose, the side of her head, her neck, and upon both eyelids. She had also bitten her lip at some point which caused damage to the inside of her mouth. She had an open wound on her cheek that had a small, semicircular abrasion near it.

As the victim still had her diamond ring on, robbery was not considered the primary motive even though her purse was taken.

The police, led by Detective Mike Hagan, sought to create a profile of the killer. They consulted with Dr. Rod Milton, a forensic psychiatrist whose profile was not released to the public.

On 9 July, Ashton's purse was found, interestingly, in Ashton Park and the woman who found the purse did not realize its significance, put it in Ashton's mailbox as stated on the papers inside of it, thus likely destroying any potential evidence that may have been on or inside the purse.

Other crimes (not murders)

On 6 June, Glover molested 77-year-old Marjorie Moseley at the Wesley Gardens Retirement Home in Belrose. She told staff that a man had put his hand under her nightgown; however, she could not identify her assailant.

Later that month, on 24 June, Glover lifted the dress of an elderly female patient at the Caroline Chisholm Nursing Home in Lane Cove and fondled her buttocks. In an adjoining room, he slid his hand down the front of another patient's nightgown and caressed her breasts. The second woman cried for help and Glover was questioned briefly before leaving.

On 8 August, Effie Carnie was assaulted on a back street in Lindfield, in Sydney's upper North Shore.

On 6 October, Glover pretended to be a physician and ran his hand up blind patient Phyllis McNeil's dress at the Wybenia Nursing Home in Neutral Bay in the lower North Shore area. McNeil called for help and Glover was neither suspected of nor identified as her molester.

Later that month on 18 October, Glover followed 86-year-old widow Doris Cox as she walked down Spit Road to her retirement village in Mosman. In a secluded stairwell at the front of the building he slammed her face into a brick wall where she fell to the ground. She was found sitting on the ground, calling for help with her face covered in blood, several scrapes on her face, and missing a few of her teeth. Luckily, Cox survived; however, she could not provide a clear description of her attacker or provide a clear recollection of what happened, likely due to her dementia. Again, neighbors washed down the area before investigators arrived, thus destroying any potential forensic evidence.

The medical examiner who conducted the autopsies on the first two victims examined Cox's injuries and concluded that they were consistent with being attacked in a similar fashion.

Margaret Pahud, 78

On 2 November, Glover approached 78-year-old Dorothy Benke while she was walking home on a backstreet just off Longueville Road in Lane Cove that was approximately ten kilometers from Mosman. He was en route to Kamilaroi Retirement Centre when he spotted Benke, for whom he offered to carry her groceries home. While initially hesitant, Benke thought that the likely 65-year-old man had a pleasant face. The talked as they walked and when they reached her house, she decided he looked harmless enough and invited him into her house for a cup of tea; however, Glover declined the tea and left, having decided that he didn't want to harm her.

After Glover left Benke's house he passed 85-year-old Margaret Pahud on her way home—also struggling with heavy grocery bags. Anger and hatred welled within him as he attacked her from behind, hitting her in the head with his hammer. She fell, face-down at his feet and he hit her again. He pulled at her dress, exposing her left breast and shoulder and then, upon hearing the sound of children's voices approaching, grabbed her purse and walked away.

This time police were certain that her assault was the work of the now-dubbed "Granny Killer" as she was hit on the back of her head with a blunt instrument and after collapsing was again struck on the side of her head. Her clothing, shoes, and cane were arranged and her handbag had been taken.

Again, there were no witnesses; however, not long after her assault a young schoolgirl found her body, thinking at first that it was simply a pile of clothing. She alerted her mother and another neighbor who rushed to the scene. Pahud was lying face-down with her head surrounded by a large pool of blood. One neighbor ran to a nearby doctor's office to seek help; however, when the physician arrived he pronounced Pahud dead.

And again, neighbors washed down the crime scene.

This time, the victim's entire purse was missing.

While the police were en route, Glover had stopped on the grounds of a nearby golf club and went through Pahud's purse. He then went to the Mosman RSL Club to spend the $300 he had stolen.

Olive Cleveland, 81

A mere 24 hours after he murdered Pahud, Glover struck up a conversation with 81-year-old Olive Cleveland as she was sitting on a bench just outside the Wesley Gardens Retirement Village (where Glover had molested Marjorie Mosely) in Belrose. At some point Cleveland became uncomfortable and got up to walk to the main building; however, Glover grabbed her from behind and forced her down a ramp into a secluded side lane where he hit her and repeatedly bashed her head into the concrete before removing her pantyhose and strangling her with them. Like the other victims, Glover rearranged her clothing, shoes, glasses, and cane and left with $60 stolen from her purse.

She was found lying face-down across the pathway and this time the killer added to his signature by pulling up her dress to expose her legs. Her pantyhose had been removed and were tied tightly around her throat, and her head was surrounded by a pool of blood.

Not unlike some of Glover's earlier victims, Cleveland's injuries were originally attributed to a fall and the crime scene was, again, washed down before police and ambulance arrived. Also again, there were no eyewitnesses.

The autopsy was eerily similar to the others. Bruising and lacerations around the head and body with cause of death attributed to strangling by her pantyhose which were tied around her neck three times.

At this point police were starting to assemble clues about the killer. To this point he always struck at around 3:00 p.m. and there were never any witnesses to the actual assaults.

The state government offered a $200,000 reward for any information about the "Granny Killer".

Muriel Falconer, 93

On 23 November, Glover was sitting in the Buena Vista Hotel on Middle Head Road in Mosman drinking a beer when he glimpsed 93-year-old widow Muriel Falconer walking across the street. Falconer was still rather active and spry for her age and she was returning from the local fruit shop, bank, other errands, and had just collected her "Meals on Wheels." It was around 5:00 p.m. Glover could feel the rage and contempt welling up inside of him.

He left his beer half-full and went to his car that he audaciously parked opposite the police station to retrieve his gloves and hammer and then followed Falconer to the exterior of her Muston Street home. From behind, he placed his hand around her mouth to silence her and then repeatedly hit her in the head and neck with his hammer.

When she fell, Glover began to remove her pantyhose; however, Falconer regained consciousness and cried for help which forced Glover to continue to hit her with the hammer until she finally stopped resisting. He removed her undergarments and strangled her with them before searching her purse and house for valuables. After rearranging her shoes, he left with $100 in stolen money.

Her body was discovered the next day by a neighbor who entered with a spare key after Meals on Wheels had not been able to get a hold of Falconer at both 11:30 a.m. and again at 1:00 p.m. The neighbor saw Falconer lying face-down in the hallway, naked from the waist down, her dress and petticoat pulled above her head, and a large pool of blood streaming from her wounds. Her shoes and bags were arranged neatly near her feet and her purse was open.

This time, however, the crime scene was intact and forensic evidence to include bloody shoeprints was able to be collected. These prints would later match Glover's shoes.

Falconer's autopsy revealed similar afflictions as the other victims of the "Granny Killer." She had been beaten, her head was fractured in three places, her face contained a number of broken bones, and her pantyhose and dress belt were wrapped tightly around her throat.

A neighbor identified the attacker as "middle-aged, portly, and grey-haired"—someone who would fit in easily into the Mosman area. The reward was increased to $250,000 by Christmas.

The task force decided to check all nearby police stations for any records of attacks upon elderly women. One report was particularly interesting: that of Margaret Todhunter who had been attacked by a grey-haired man who was "50 years of age, well-kept, broad shoulders, thick chest, large stomach, and who wore a white business shirt and cream trousers" who grabbed her bag. This description fit Glover to a tee.

Daisy Roberts, 82 (not murdered)

After Muriel Falconer's murder, Glover visited the Greenwich Hospital on River Road on one of his pie sales rounds on 11 January 1990. He entered the hospital's palliative care ward where he found four elderly, ill women including 82-year-old advanced cancer patient Daisy Roberts (who has since passed away). While in his work uniform and carrying a clipboard, Glover asked Roberts if she "was losing any body heat" before pulling up her nightgown and "touch[ing] her in an indecent manner".

Roberts called for help and this time hospital sister Pauline Davis saw Glover in the ward. She confronted him and he ran; however, Davis was able to record his car's license number and called the police. This time, also, hospital staff was able to both name and identify Glover as he was already known from his pie rounds.

One week later the police returned with a photograph of Glover and both Davis and Roberts were able to positively identify him. While this was, indeed, a significant breakthrough, the hospital assaults were not as of yet linked to the "Granny Killer" murders. Compounding the problem was that said assaults were not reported to the murder task force for three weeks.

Instead, detectives from Chatswood Police Station contacted Glover and requested he attend an interview at the station the following day. Of course, he failed to appear and police subsequently called his home and were informed by his wife that he had attempted suicide via overdose and was recovering at the Royal North Shore Hospital. At the hospital, Glover declined to be interviewed; however, he did permit police to take a Polaroid photograph of him. This was the photo that police had shown to Davis and Roberts.

Hospital staff also handed the police a handwritten suicide note from Glover on a sheet of Four 'n' Twenty Pies letterhead that said, "no more grannies ... grannies" and "Essie started it"—Essie being Glover's mother-in-law, Veronica Rolls, who had lived with her daughter and son-in-law for 13 years before moving into a nursing home in 1988. She ultimately died on 21 January 1989. Glover's own mother had also recently passed away on 11 October 1988. Experts believe that these deaths were a catalyst for his murders in addition to a deep-seated hatred of his mother for leaving his father and remarrying coupled with an equally intense hatred of his mother-in-law.

It took two more weeks before the note and the photo were given to the task force assembled to catch Australia's first serial killer.

Glover was interviewed over the nursing home assaults and denied all accusations. Since police had limited evidence they decided not to question him about the murders because, they believed, that it would make Glover aware of police suspicions against him. Instead, he was placed under constant surveillance with an automatic tracking device. To evade potential followers, Glover would drive around the block more than once or drive the wrong way up one-way streets. Had the police done their job properly, Glover's last victim might still be alive today.

Joan Sinclair, 60

Glover's last victim was 60-year-old divorcee Joan Sinclair from Beauty Point, Mosman, with whom Glover had been having a relationship. On 19 March 1990, while police had him under surveillance, he went to visit his lover who let him into her home at approximately 10:00 a.m. By 1:00 p.m. there had been no sign of Glover or any movement inside of the house.

Later in the afternoon two boys attempted to enter the house but the gate was locked. They sought assistance from a neighbor to no avail. Additionally, a dog barking inside the house indicated something was not quite right. At approximately 5:00 p.m., the surveillance team became concerned and obtained permission to enter the house at 6:00 p.m.

Two uniformed officers knocked on the front door to no avail. They saw through the rear glass door a hammer lying in a pool of dried blood atop a mat. Four detectives searched the house and found Sinclair's battered head wrapped in a bundle of blood-slaked towels. She was nude from the waist down and her pantyhose were tied around her neck. This time, her genitals showed signs of damage; however, Glover denied sexually assaulting her.

After finding Sinclair's body they searched for Glover who was later discovered unconscious in a filled bathtub. He was transported to Royal North Shore Hospital and placed under police guard.

Sinclair's cause of death was due to multiple head wounds from the claw hammer found at the scene. Despite some dissimilarities between her murder and the other murders, police believed there was ample evidence to suggest that they were all linked and that Glover was the perpetrator.

Glover told police he murdered Sinclair and explained their relationship which he claimed had been ongoing for some time. He admitted to beating her head with his hammer, removing her pantyhose, and strangling her with them. He then admitted to rolling her body onto a mat before wrapping four towels around her head to reduce the blood flow, and then dragging her lifeless body across the floor. He then claimed to have run the bath and taken a handful of Valium with a bottle of Vat 69 before slashing his left wrist and lying down in the bath to die. Police were, in fact, relieved that Glover lived so they wouldn't have to speculate forever as to whether he was the "Granny Killer" or not.

Investigation and Arrest

By January 1990, Glover had been on his murderous rampage for ten months and had already murdered five elderly women and assaulted several more in hospitals and nursing homes. Each victim had been attacked within a few kilometers of the Greenwich Hospital, and one had been murdered a mere 250 meters from the hospital's front gate.

As previously mentioned, despite assemblage of a massive police task force consisting of 70 officers the previous November to catch Australia's first serial killer, alarm bells failed to go off when police botched their chance to question Glover and obtain a search warrant for his house and car. Had they obtained a warrant, they would have discovered the gloves and hammer under his front seat. Instead, police called Glover to ask him to come in for an interview on 13 January.

Thus, police have been subject to scathing criticisms from a number of sources because had they acted in a timely manner then Sinclair might still be alive today.

When confronted with the evidence against him, Glover admitted to the murders; however, he denied responsibility for other crimes in which he was the prime suspect such as the 1977 murder of Florence Broadhurst in Paddington.

In sum, he was charged with 14 offenses: six counts of first-degree murder, one count of attempted murder, one count of robbery with wounding, one count of robbery, four counts of indecent assault, and one count of assaulting a female.

Trial and Conviction

Glover's trial began on 28 March 1990 in which he pled not guilty on the grounds of diminished responsibility. One psychiatrist who evaluated Glover testified that he had built up hostility and aggression against his mother since he was a child, and then against his mother-in-law who was called his "trigger". When his mother-in-law died, Glover felt he had to take out his aggression against a surrogate. The psychiatrist also stated that the very few mass murderers in Australia are perpetrated by mentally ill perpetrators who oftentimes have some organic brain disease; however, at the time of his crimes Glover was completely sane. He was described as an anger-retaliatory predator with narcissistic tendencies despite outwardly being a "nice guy" with a "normal" life.

Thus, the prosecutor maintained throughout the trial that Glover was, indeed, fully aware of his actions because when he killed his victims he was planning how he would spend the victims' money, not to mention that he took time to clean his hammer with acid to destroy any potential biological evidence. As Glover was impotent and had zero interest in sex, his ritualistic strangulation of his victims with pantyhose was done to trick the police into thinking that the murderer was sexually motivated.

Compounding the problem was that Glover was seriously addicted to poker machines and the best way for him to obtain more money with which to gamble was to steal it.

On 29 November 1990, Glover was found guilty and after the verdict was delivered, presiding Judge James Wood stressed Glover's dangerousness. He said, "[Glover] is able to choose when to attack and when to stay his hand. He is cunning and able to cover his tracks. It is plain that he has chosen his moments carefully. Although the crimes have been opportunistic, he has not gone in where the risks were overwhelming".

Wood added that Glover's crimes involved "extreme violence inflicted on elderly women, accompanied by theft or robbery of their property" thus making Glover "exceedingly dangerous" and this opinion was mirrored by the psychiatrists who proffered testimony at his trial.

Sentence

Thus, due to Wood's sentiments attesting to Glover's dangerousness, he said, "I have no alternative other than to impose the maximum available sentence, which means that the prisoner will be required to spend the remainder of his natural life in Jail. It is inappropriate to express any date as to release on parole. Having regard to those life sentences, this is not a case where the prisoner may ever be released pursuant to order of this court. He is never to be released".

After being sentenced to life without any possibility of parole, Glover expressed that his only concern was that he would never see the ocean again. He failed to demonstrate much emotion as Wood handed down his sentence.

Aftermath

After his convictions, Glover admitted that he "never worried about who his victims were, or why he killed them" and that he wanted to stop but could not.

Glover committed suicide in prison by hanging himself (his third known attempt). The 72-year-old "Granny Killer" was found hanging from a shower rail in his cell in Lithgow Prison in New South Wales.

Prior to doing so, he handed his last visitor a sketch of a park with a number of changes in the sketch which Glover pointed out. In the sketch were two palm trees; in the middle of the right one was the number "nine" composed of leaves and branches. The number nine is said to represent the number of murders that Glover committed—or the number of unsolved murders he likely also committed. The nine additional victims/unsolved cases include: Elsie Boyes, 63, 3 June 1967, in Prahran; Emmie May Anderson, 78, 19 October 1961, in East Melbourne; Irene Kiddle, 61, 22 March 1963, in Saint Kilda; Christina Yankos, 63, 9 April 1968, in Albert Park; Florence Broadhurst, 78, 16 October 1977, in Paddington; Josephine McDonald, 72, 29 August 1984, in Ettalong; Wanda Amundsen, 83, 21 November 1986, in Umina; as well as two other unknown victims.

THE TRUCK STOP KILLER

ANA BENSON

49

The United States is known for long desolate highways and interstates. Designed to make traveling easier and faster, thousands of vehicles go down these roads on a daily basis. During the 1960s and 1970s, seeing hitchhikers was nothing unusual. But not every one of them got to their desired destination. The number of missing hitchhikers made people change their minds about this type of travel. It became very risky in the second half of the 1970s, and parents started warning their children about the dangers that loom on the interstates. After all, it is impossible to know the person who picks you up or their intentions.

Robert Ben Rhoades became a truck driver in the 1980s. He was a disturbed individual who saw his new employment as a perfect hunting ground. After all, the victims would come to him, asking for a ride. He was known nationwide as The Truck Stop Killer. While the total number of his victims is still unconfirmed, Rhoades was one of the most dangerous serial killers because he was driven by his sexual fantasies and the need to dominate.

Early life

Robert Ben Rhoades was born on November 22nd, 1945 in Council Bluffs, Iowa. Since his father was an officer in the US Army and was stationed in West Germany at the time, Robert Ben Rhoades was raised by his mother. His father was discharged from the army a couple of years later while Rhoades was in elementary school. According to his peers, Rhoades was a good student who loved learning and was involved in numerous extracurricular activities. He was a member of a choir and excelled at the French language. Not to forget that Rhoades was also interested in sports such as football and wrestling. It appears that he had an average upbringing without any indications of verbal or physical abuse by the people who were close to him.

The first signs of trouble appeared when Rhoades was sixteen years old. He was arrested for tampering with a vehicle. It was very likely that Rhoades was attempting to steal the said car. He was once again arrested a year later for public fighting. While this can be seen as a typical teenage behavior, it was very unlike Rhoades to break the law. His grades didn't change too much, and Rhoades graduated from Monticello High School in 1964. Inspired by his father's service in the US Army, Rhoades enlisted in Marine Corps immediately after the graduation. But his family life took a strange turn that same year.

Rhoades' father was arrested for sexually assaulting and molesting a 12 years old girl. He took his own life while waiting for the trial. It is still unclear whether Rhoades' father abused his son while he was young, but it is evident that the death of a parent did have an impact on Rhoades. His personality changed, and he just wasn't into Marine Corps anymore. Rhoades was dishonorably discharged sometime around 1967 or 1968 because he participated in a robbery. He saw this as a chance to earn a college diploma, so he enrolled into a university in 1969. His enthusiasm for learning was short-lived, and Rhoades dropped out soon after.

Even though Rhoades was a promising young man, he simply lost his spark. After leaving the college, he tried to join the law enforcement, but that didn't go well either. He was rejected due to his previous arrests and the dishonorable discharge from the Marine Corps. Rhoades moved back to Council Bluffs with a plan to start a family. He continued to work low paying jobs in the 1970s. Rhoades was married to his first wife for a total of four years, and they had a son together. Immediately after their divorce, he decided to tie the knot once again. Rhoades quickly divorced his second wife as well, after meeting his future third wife, Deborah. Eventually, he started working as a long-haul truck driver sometime during the 1980s. He became profoundly interested in BDSM scene which was becoming more mainstream in that decade. It would be later discovered that Rhoades abused his third wife, beating her on a regular basis.

The combination of his interest in BDSM and the fact that he was a long-haul truck driver inspired him to turn his vehicle into a mobile torture chamber. Robert Ben Rhoades was always on the move, traveling across the United States on a regular basis. This allowed him to pick up hitchhikers or sex workers, torture them, and then disappear without leaving a trace.

Kidnapping and the first murders

Robert Ben Rhoades saw his job as a truck driver as an opportunity to explore his darkest fantasies. Having in mind that he customized his sleeper cab into a torture chamber means that he did prepare for the murders months before putting his plan into work. He was cautious about the victim selection as well, focusing on the hitchhikers who were transients or runaways, as well as sex workers who frequented truck stops all over the country. It would take months or even years for someone to report a missing hitchhiker, and the same goes for sex workers who often had a drug problem and lived far away from their families.

On February 5th, 1990, a girl appeared on the side of a road in Houston, Texas. She was apparently in distress, with numerous bruises all over her body. The girl was trying to get help, and one driver finally stopped his car. He drove her to a payphone, and the girl contacted the law enforcement. She was taken to a Houston Police Station where she told the officers about the horrors she endured. The girl was eighteen years old, and she was from California. She wanted to hitchhike across the country and knew that the best way to find a ride is to ask a truck driver to give her a lift. The girl approached a man at a truck stop, and he told her that he is going through Arizona that night. She climbed into a cabin and fell asleep a couple of hours later.

The girl was woken up when the man started tying her up in the back of the cabin. The driver who introduced himself as Dustin chained the girl, then continued to torture her by piercing her skin and beating her with a whip. He also sexually assaulted her. The torture continued for six days until they arrived in Houston. The truck driver took her to his apartment and tied her to the bed, continuing the abuse. He then cut her hair short and brought her back to his truck. But he failed to tie up the chains correctly, so the girl saw this as an opportunity for an escape. She was sure that the man will not let her walk away and that he would very likely kill her soon.

Once the truck driver stopped the vehicle to pick up a new load, the girl bolted out of the cabin, running to the street. She did give the officers a good description of the truck, and they began the search. The police stopped one vehicle, but the girl told them that they got it wrong. Of course, the officers checked the driver's background, and since he had no criminal record, he was released. The girl asked the law enforcement to stop searching for her rapist because she will not be filing any charges. Her statement was: "I don't see any good in filing charges. It's just going to be my word against his. If there were any evidence, I would file. I would file charges and sue him." All she wanted to do is get back home to California and try to forget this horror ever happened. It was more than evident that she was still afraid of her attacker, and that was understandable having in mind everything she went through. She did manage to escape, but others will not be that lucky.

Rhoades' first confirmed murders were a couple of hitchhikers. He picked up Candace Walsh and Douglas Zyskowski in January of 1990 somewhere in Texas while he was traveling cross country. Seeing Douglas as a threat, Rhoades killed him shortly after the couple got into his truck. He shot him and left his body in Sutton County, Texas. Rhoades then placed Candace into his torture chamber where she was tortured and repeatedly raped for an entire week. As his drive was coming to an end, Rhoades knew that he had to kill the girl and get rid of her body. He did so in Millard County, Utah.

The case of Regina Kay Walters

On February 5th, 1990, Regina Kay Walters who was fourteen years old at the time, and her eighteen years old boyfriend Ricky Lee Jones were hitchhiking in Pasadena, Texas. Regina came from a broken home, and her parents were divorced. She sometimes stayed with her father in Houston, Texas, but this time Regina was visiting her mother. The couple was attempting to run away from home and were relieved when a truck stopped by the highway to give them a lift. Regina's mother came home later that evening after a long day at work. She was surprised to find the house empty, and her daughter wasn't anywhere in the neighborhood. She searched for a note or a message but found none. Then she called her ex-husband in Houston, hoping that he knew the whereabouts of their daughter. He was clueless and haven't heard from Regina in days.

After speaking to Regina's friends, she determined that her daughter is missing. Pasadena Police Department was informed about it, and the mother provided them with the description. The detectives spoke to Regina's mother who told them she did argue with her daughter the night before she disappeared. There was a possibility Regina might have run away from home, but she would probably call her mother by now. Detective Susanne Jackson who had a lot of experience in finding juvenile runaways took the case. She advised the mother to continue putting up posters all over the town in hopes someone might have seen something or knew the location of her daughter.

The posers did list a phone number and a reward for anyone who provided useful information to the police. One caller told them that Regina was seen talking with two local boys Ricky and Billy. The second caller gave an address at which he had seen Regina two nights before the disappearance. Police went there and discovered that a man named Billy was renting that particular apartment. They had their first lead but had no idea where to find Billy. Detective Jackson casually mentioned to her colleagues that she was trying to locate two boys called Ricky and Billy, and they immediately connected the dots. The police were after the two of them for stealing a car, so now everyone was on a lookout. Billy was caught near the apartment where he lived with his girlfriend. They still couldn't find Ricky Lee Jones.

When interviewed by the police about Regina, he told them that she was dating his friend Ricky and that the two decided to run away to Mexico. They were very much in love, and Regina wanted to live with Ricky. Since Ricky had family south of the border, they decided to head out there. Ricky Lee Jones was a problematic teenager, and Regina had no prior misdemeanors. The police now knew that they hitchhiked to Mexico, but their whereabouts were still unknown. The detectives decided to enter Regina's description into NCIC, hoping that she might be located by the law enforcement in a different state.

The detectives traveled to Houston to interview Regina's father. He told them that his phone rang on the evening of March 17th and a man asked him if he is Regina's father. When he confirmed it, the man continued the conversation by saying that he knew where Regina is. The unknown caller told Regina's father that she is in a barn and that her hair is cut short. Then he hung up the phone. The odd thing is that the number was unlisted in a phonebook and it wasn't written on the missing person posters that were distributed all over Texas. After hearing about the strange phone call, detective Jackson contacted the phone company and asked them to trace the location of the caller. The results came in a week later, and now the police knew that the call originated from a payphone in Ennis, Texas.

As the weeks went by, it was clear to the law enforcement that something terrible happened to Regina Kay Walters. The teen couldn't be located and having in mind the cryptic phone call her father received, detective Jackson who was working the case was sure that they would not find Regina alive. Her boyfriend, Ricky Lee Jones, was the prime suspect due to the lack of evidence proving otherwise. Months passed before the police finally caught a break in the case. A farmer living in Bond County, Illinois was getting ready to burn down his old farmhouse. The structure hasn't been used in years, and he wanted to remove it from his property. The man went inside just to make sure there was nothing of value in there, and as he walked around the farmhouse, he noticed something unusual. He approached a pile of hay and saw skeleton remains of a human body. He ran out of the building and phoned the police right away.

The law enforcement got to the scene and analyzed it. It was apparent that the body was there for quite some time. There were no items of clothing in the barn, and they couldn't find an ID. The corpse did have a wire around the neck, and a couple of strains of short hair remained on the skull. The body was small, so the investigators assumed that the victim was a child. Bond Country didn't have a murder in years and the locals were shocked. There were no missing persons that fit the age of the corpse anywhere near the location, so the police assumed it was dumped there. Since Bond County is close to the interstate 70, the victim could have arrived from anywhere.

The coroner did an excellent job in helping to identify the victim. He told the Illinois State Police that the corpse was female, probably a teenager and that her hair was recently cut short. She was strangled in a very violent manner because the killer tightened the wire around her neck sixteen times, almost beheading the girl. The lead detective from Illinois State Police entered the information into the database of the missing persons and narrowed down the results. He then sent the description of their unidentified victim to the agencies working the cases. It reached the police station in Pasadena, Texas and they called Illinois right away. One detail that stood out was the location at which the body was found. Detective Jackson remembered the phone call made to Regina's father months before because the man was talking about a barn.

She started communicating with the Illinois State Police, and they exchanged the information quickly. Detective Jackson sent Regina's dental records, and they were a match. The body which was found in Illinois was indeed Regina Kay Walters. Ricky was still the primary suspect at that point, but the crime scene analysis determined that whoever committed this crime knew what they were doing. Ricky simply didn't have enough experience to execute a murder like this. The police officers did create a profile of a murderer, and the fact that the interstate was near the barn told them that they should search for a truck driver or a traveler who is always on the road. It was clear that the perpetrator was a sadist who enjoyed torturing his victims before killing them.

Ricky Lee Jones' body was discovered on March 3rd, 1991 in Lamar County, Mississippi. He was dumped near a river, and his body was almost completely decomposed. But the gunshot wound on his head was very noticeable, so the authorities knew the cause of death right away. No physical evidence was found near the corpse. It was clear that Ricky was killed around the time of Regina's abduction. His remains were unidentified until 2008 because the police didn't have any DNA for comparison. The police had no other leads, and the case wasn't moving anywhere. The detectives did have a profile of the killer, so they knew that he would murder again, but catching someone who is always on the road is very challenging.

Catching Rhoades

On April 1st, 1990, officer Mike Miller who worked for Arizona Highway Patrol was doing his usual routine on interstate 10 when he noticed a parked truck. The hazard lights were on, and the officer thought that the driver might be in trouble. Plus, the truck was parked near a ramp, so he had to move the vehicle as soon as possible. Officer Miller got out of his car and approached the truck. He knocked on the cabin door, and the man jumped out, raising his hands in the air. The officer could hear a female voice coming from the back of the cabin. The man claimed that everything was alright, but the woman continued to scream, asking for help. The officer took the truck driver back to his patrol car, and he handcuffed him. He went back to see if the woman was alright and was shocked to find her tied. Officer Miller called for backup because he suspected that the truck was a scene of a crime. Casa Grande was the nearest town, so the local law enforcement arrived to investigate the possible kidnapping.

When they climbed into the sleeper cab, they found a full torture chamber with chains and hooks. Additionally, the police discovered a briefcase filled with different instruments, as well as a camera. They identified the driver as Robert Ben Rhoades. Judging by the looks of his truck, the police was sure that he had done similar crimes in the past. He was arrested and placed in the custody. The woman was interviewed by the detectives, and she told them that Rhoades picked her up at a truck stop near Phoenix, Arizona just a couple of hours before the highway patrol officer found her. She fell asleep during the ride, and the next thing she could remember was that she was tied up and Rhoades was sexually assaulting her. The woman was speckled with bruises, but she did tell the investigators that she tried to defend herself by biting Rhoades.

Unfortunately, the woman did have a history of mental illness, so the detectives knew that her story would not hold up in court. Rhoades gave his version of the events and claimed that the sexual encounter was consensual. But he did have the bite mark on his neck. Detectives were aware that they needed to investigate Rhoades further. The lead investigator started going through the similar crimes which were reported across the United States. Police officers from Houston, Texas did hear about the Arizona case and remembered the assault from January 1990. Rhoades fit the description which was given to the police. The nature of the crime was very similar as well because it included bondage and torture.

The law enforcement from Arizona was given the warrant to search Rhoades apartment in Houston, Texas. They discovered numerous torture devices and bondage equipment. Their goal was to find evidence that Rhoades was a serial rapist because they were still in the dark about his murders. As they went through the apartment, they discovered bloody towels and plenty of photographs of two short-haired women. In some photos, the women were tied up, so the detectives thought that the images were taken by Rhoades to serve as souvenirs. However, they failed to identify the women. Thus the search didn't provide them with possible witnesses.

Identifying the victims

Keeping Rhoades locked up was a real challenge since his kidnap victim from Arizona wasn't credible, and her story would very likely be dismissed in the court. The prosecution just couldn't make a solid case that will place Rhoades behind bars for good. They offered him a deal – Rhoades would be in prison for a total of six years with time served and would be eligible for parole after one year. All he needed to do is plead guilty to the assault. Rhoades accepted the deal, thinking that he did outsmart the law enforcement once again.

But he didn't know that the Illinois State Police asked the FBI for help in solving the Regina Kay Walters murder. The agents began combing the database for other cases that would fit the modus operandi of their suspect. One FBI agent was present in Houston, Texas when the bruised woman with chopped hair was interviewed after escaping from a truck driver. The police did stop a truck driver called Bob Rhoades that day, but the woman refused to identify him, and she dropped the charges.

The FBI knew they were onto something when the detective from Houston shared information that Rhoades was in custody of Arizona State Police because he raped and assaulted a woman in that state. The agent contacted the law enforcement over there, and they told him about the search of Rhoades' apartment. When they mentioned the strange photographs of a woman in a barn, the FBI agent knew that he possibly had cracked the case. The barn photos were sent to him immediately, and he began to compare them with Regina's family photos. They were a match. The black dress that was worn by Regina in the photos was found in Rhoades' apartment during the search. There was a second set of photos that depicted a different woman, and she will be later identified as Candace Walsh. Robert Ben Rhoades was responsible for the murder of Regina Kay Walters, and he will not be getting out of the prison so soon if they manage to build a solid case against him.

After going through the items collected at Rhoades' residence, the officers found Regina's notebook that contained her father's unlisted number. The FBI agents went to Rhoades' employee, and he provided them with the data regarding his truck deliveries. One receipt proved that he was in Ennis, Texas on the day the call to Regina's father was made. Since Rhoades worked as a truck driver for years, the FBI agents entered the information in VICAP to find other possible victims, and they got over fifty results that matched his movement during that time frame.

The police got another warrant to search Rhoades' truck, and the crime scene investigators discovered Regina's hair and fingerprints, alongside other physical evidence. That was enough to prove that the girl was in Rhoades' vehicle at some point. Since Rhoades was just days away from his release in Arizona, FBI convinced the detectives to press charges for kidnapping and murder in Bond County, Illinois. They hoped that Rhoades would confess everything as soon as he speaks with the Illinois State Police but they were wrong. He remained confident and denied any involvement in the crime.

The trial and the aftermath

The trial started in 1993 after a delay because Rhoades' defense was building the case. He was extradited from Arizona to Illinois where he was charged with the first-degree murder of Regina Kay Walters. The trial lasted for several months, and Robert Ben Rhoades was found guilty of first-degree murder. The sentence was life without parole. He was to serve his sentence in Menard Correctional Center in Chester, Illinois.

Rhoades was back in the courtroom in 2005 when he was extradited to Utah. He was supposed to go on trial for the murders of Candace Walsh and Douglas Zyskowski. However, their families decided not to go through it all and dropped the charges. But since the crime was committed in Texas, Rhoades was transported there, and the trial was set to begin. Rhoades pleaded guilty to avoid the death penalty in that state. He received another life sentence for the murder of Walsh and Zyskowski. Rhoades is still serving his sentences in Menard Correctional Center.

THE ICE KILLER : THE TRUE STORY OF ROBERT HANSEN

62

EZRA GILCHRIST

Robert Hansen was dubbed the "Butcher Baker" by the media after he kidnapped, raped and killed at least seventeen women with possibly more victims that have yet to be identified. The murders took place in and around his hometown of Anchorage, Alaska as Hansen would hunt down his victims in the woods with a variety of weapons. It would take over twelve years before authorities would finally capture and convict Hansen in 1983. His case would remain out of the limelight until a movie called "Frozen Ground" would be released, detailing his exploits with John Cusack starring as Hansen.

EARLY YEARS

Hansen was born to Danish immigrants in Estherville, Iowa in 1939. Both of his parents were strict and Robert would be crippled by shyness for his entire life. He had a stutter and a bad case of acne which left pockmarks on both of his cheeks. His father, Christian, was a baker and Robert would eventually follow him into the same occupation. But his father was not a positive influence on him, routinely belittling his son. Robert had no escape, he was bullied both at home and at school.

At school, he was the proverbial social outcast. He would walk down the halls with his eyes downcast and very few people even noticed him. He only had a small handful of male friends who kept him at arm's length and virtually no female friends.

He had no success whatsoever with the opposite sex, being alternately ignored and ridiculed. This rejection would evolve into a seething hatred of all attractive women as his sexual fantasies about them turned into violent ones.

With no outlet, he took up hunting and found solace in the woods, shooting at animals.

At the age of eighteen, Robert would join the United States Army Reserve and would serve for one year before being discharged. The army service would give him a bit of self-confidence as Robert now attempted to talk to women and ask for dates. But women were taken aback by his awkward nature, his stutter and his thousand-mile stare behind black-rimmed glasses.

With his military experience, he would find employment at a police academy in Pocahontas, Iowa as an assistant drill instructor. Once there, he began badgering a secretary for a date until she filed a complaint against him. He would eventually meet his first wife in Pocahontas, marrying her in the summer of 1960.

The marriage would not last. Only a few months later, Robert would be arrested for burning down a school bus garage.

The bullying and torment Hansen experienced during his high school years would prove to be too much. He had to somehow, someway get back at his tormentors. So even three years after he graduated he decided to go back to his old school and burn down the garage that housed the school bus.

He would be sentenced to three years in jail during which his wife would file for divorce. He would serve a little over twenty months before being released.

The arson episode would prove to be another step on the ladder to Hansen's eventual homicidal psychosis. He was showing all of the earmarks of a serial killer; arson and cruelty to animals. He had felt powerless his whole life but would act out in fantasies where he would have power...whether it was by starting a fire or shooting a deer. Eventually, this need for power would lead him to a deep-seated desire to have power over the women who rejected him throughout his life.

ESCALATING BEHAVIOR

Robert would test the waters of criminal behavior starting with petty thefts. He would be arrested several times for theft, looking to be growing into a small time criminal until1963 when he married his second wife.

Four years into their marriage, the couple would have two children and move to Anchorage, Alaska.

Robert would start work in a local bakery. Under his father's tutelage, he was a capable baker and hiring him was a no-brainer. But his co-workers found him to be a social misfit. He would brag to them about the strangest things, like his kleptomania and ability to steal things without getting caught.

JUST ANOTHER FACE IN THE CROWD

Hansen went out of his way to give off the appearance of a respectable citizen.

His neighbors liked him and he would set several hunting records in the area, decorating his home with the heads of big game and fish. He would open his own bakery in a downtown mini-mall, becoming friends with the regular customers and even servicing the policemen who came in for their morning donut.

No one, not his wife, children or his neighbors knew of the monster that lurked inside him.

But he couldn't keep the monster hidden long. In fact, the respectable front was just camouflage.

In 1967, Hansen would assault a young receptionist at gunpoint. He would plead no contest to the assault charge but serve very little time. A few months later, he followed a pretty eighteen-year-old girl home and again tried to sexually assault her.

He would serve very little time in jail, being sent instead to a psychiatric facility where he described his bizarre and dark sexual fantasies. He would tell his psychiatrist that he suffered from memory lapses and remembered little of what took place during his assaults.

The courts were lenient on Hansen to a fault.

In 1971, Hansen would kidnap and rape a seventeen-year-old waitress outside a coffee shop.

He would let her go but not without a threat.

"I will hunt you down," he hissed in her ear. "Hunt you down and kill you. I'm a respectable man. I own a business. You're just a kid. No one will believe you."

The teenage girl, scared out of her wits, believed him.

With no punishment or capture in sight, Hansen would become even bolder as he plotted out his mouth violent fantasies.

FIRST BLOOD

In what would seem to be a recurring theme for Hansen's victims, there was very little media coverage or follow-up investigations.

In 1973, a seventeen-year-old schoolgirl named Megan Emerick walked out of a dorm laundry room in Seward, Alaska and disappeared without a trace.

She is presumed to have been another of Hansen's victims though he would later deny it.

Unfortunately, Megan's disappearance would garner little in the way of press or law enforcement investigation. There were a few fliers and short articles in the local newspaper but little else offered.

Megan was a quiet girl who grew up in the peaceful town of Delta Junction. She liked to go out on the Yukon River to hunt and fish. A typical teenager, she liked rock music and horses but she left home at an early age to go to the Seward Skill Center, a place in Alaska where she would learn a vocation.

But on July 7th, she would disappear.

Years later, the vanishing teenage girls would be part of a growing trend in the Eklutna and Knik River areas.

LOST IN THE FOG

As construction of an eight-hundred-mile oil pipeline began in Alaska, a different population began filing into Anchorage. The oil money brought in prostitutes, pimps, and drug dealers who sought to service the oil workers who now had money to burn. The community began a transient one and sudden disappearances became nothing out of the ordinary. Anchorage became a frontier town, a city full of strangers where people disappeared without a trace.

Robert would initially target any woman who caught his eye. But he began to learn that strippers and prostitutes were less likely to have people come looking for them. He would soon develop his own modus operandi, a system that he would adhere to with religious fervor.

He would target solitary women under the guise that he was a photographer, offering compensation if they posed for him. Hansen would then arrange a meeting place in a coffee shop and wait outside, making sure that the woman arrived alone. Once assured that there would be no witness, he would arrive at the coffee shop and convince the woman to come leave with him for the photo shoot. They would get into the car and he would already have one-half of the handcuff attached to the passenger side drive handle. Once he got into the driver side, he would lean over and in one motion handcuff their wrist and take out the gun from his glove compartment.

Sometimes he would drive the women home or to an isolated motel room where he would rape them. Other times he would fly to a desolate area along the Knik River.

A STRANGE CODE

Robert didn't kill all of his victims. Sometimes he would rape them and release the ones who he thought really found him attractive. His reasoning was, they played out to his fantasy and didn't deserve to die.

Others, the ones who resisted and fought, he would pretend to set free. Then he would hunt them down through the woods and shoot them with his rifle.

By the summer of 1980, bodies of dead prostitutes began to be found in and around the Anchorage area. But finding dead bodies in the Alaska wilderness was not an out of the ordinary type thing. Hikers would often get lost in the wilderness and not know how to make their way back, succumbing to the elements.

The first would be a young woman believed to be in her late teens or early twenties. Workers in a building found a shallow grave on Eklutna Lake Road. The body was badly decomposed and half-eaten by bears. Police were able to make a facial reconstruction from the skull and published their approximation of the young woman's appearance to the local news outlets. The victim was never identified, however, and to this day is still known as "Eklutna Annie."

When her body was recovered, she was estimated to be in her late teens or early twenties. She was between 4'11" and 5'3" inches tall with long, reddish-brown hair. Hansen would admit that she was the first victim that he killed but that he didn't know her name.

Hansen said that she or her family lived in Kodiak. Investigators believed that she may have come from Washington or California.

What is certain is that she was a topless dancer or a prostitute that Hansen picked up, offering to pay for her services. He told her that he lived in Muldoon but when Hansen drove past the town the woman panicked. She tried to escape out of his truck but Hansen pulled a gun on her.

"Now look," Hansen said. "If you do exactly what I tell you and don't give me any problem whatsoever, there's going to be none, you won't get hurt in any way, shape or form."

"Eklutna Annie" could only nod in agreement out of fear. They continued to drive, her heart racing with fear, her mind racing with strategies on how she could escape.

But then Hansen's truck got lodged in the wet Alaska mud. Hansen allowed the young woman to step out of the vehicle to help put the truck back on solid ground.

Then she ran.

Hansen stated that he caught her by the hair as she took a knife out from her purse.

Overpowering the young girl, Hansen wrenched the knife away and stabbed her in the back.

Her body would be found on July 21st, 1980 buried near a power line.

MORE BODIES...

Joanne Messina was another body found near Eklutna Lake Road, buried in a gravel pit. Her body was badly decomposed and there was little evidence remaining. She worked as a topless dancer as did other Hansen victims such as Sherry Morrow and Paula Goulding.

Sherry Morrow was a striking beauty, with feathered blonde hair and heart-shaped lips. She was an aspiring model who turned to topless dancing to make ends meet. Like he would do so many times, Hansen would meet her under the guise of a photo shoot.

Sherry would be among the first that Hansen would play the "hunting game" with. After raping and torturing her, he flew her to the woods where he sent her blindfolded and handcuffed, telling her to run.

His sadistic fantasies now coming to life, Hansen would hunt her down. He would follow her through the woods as she cried and begged for her life.

He shot her in the back, rolled her over and ripped off a necklace from her neck.

A 'good luck' arrowhead locket that her boyfriend had given her.

It was the next step in his mind, to begin taking mementos and trophies of his victims. He would set them aside in a box then when he felt the need to relive the moment he could take the souvenir out, fingering it through his hands and relive the fantasies in his mind.

UPPING THE ANTE...

The adrenaline high that Hansen got when he first began killing started to subside. So he began the 'hunting game' in order to feed the monster inside. He had gone from petty theft to attempted sexual assault before graduating to rape and murder.

Now it was turning the rape and murder into a sport.

Sherry's body would be found on the banks of the Knik River. Sherry had been reported missing for over a year and her body was found in a shallow grave on the banks of the river. Two off-duty police officers were in the wilderness hunting moose when they came upon her decomposed remains. She had been shot in the back three times with what investigators believed to have been a hunting rifle. Her body was fully clothed but there were no bullet holes in her clothing. Investigators believe that she had been naked when Hansen shot her after which he put her clothes back on.

Police were able to identify Sherry's body from dental records. She had been reported missing over a year ago by her boyfriend. The clothes they had found on her skeletal remains were the same as the clothes described by her boyfriend.

The case would go nowhere, however. The police told the boyfriend that the killer had over a year to cover his tracks. Finding him would be next to impossible.

Paula Goulding would meet the same fate as Sherry Morrow. Only seventeen-years-old and looking for work, the unemployed secretary started work as an exotic dancer to pay her rent. She would be targeted by Hansen and fall victim to him in the same way Sherry did. He would capture her, send her into the wilderness blindfolded where he would chase her down then after she couldn't run anymore, shoot her down like an animal.

Paula's body had been found in the exact same fashion, shot in the back but then redressed after death.

Sue Luna's body would be found two years later, the young Asian woman was forced to strip herself naked while Hansen made her run like a dog through the woods. The game was intoxicating to him as he shot her in the back after a lengthy chase.

Delynn Frey, Teresa Watson, Angela Feddern, Tamara Pederson, Lisa Futrell, and Andrea Altiery would all become victims of Hansen. He would collect "trophies" from each of them, taking a custom-made fish necklace from Andrea Altiery that would later be a critical piece of evidence when he would be captured.

But that capture when not come until June 13th, 1983 when Hansen encountered seventeen-year-old prostitute Cindy Paulson.

A STREET SMART STREETWALKER

Hansen was trolling for his next victim when he spotted Cindy selling her wares on an empty street. He had enticed Cindy to come into his car for $200 in exchange for oral sex. Cindy didn't feel threatened by the man, she got into his car without a second thought. Before she knew it, however, he handcuffed her to the and held a wood handled revolver to her head.

"Not a s-s-s-sound," the man stuttered as he put the car into drive. He drove her to his home in Muldoon. The alert Cindy began taking notes in her mind. The home was in a relatively well-to-do area. Once she entered, she found the home to be well kept and with nice furniture and full of hunting trophies. Hansen took her down to his den where there was a chain hanging from the ceiling. He tied her to the chain and stripped off her clothes. He would hold her captive for hours, alternating between raping and physically torturing her.

Hansen would grow tired and chained her by the neck to a post in the basement. Hansen then laid on the couch and went to sleep.

Upon awakening, Hansen untied Cindy and threw her in his car.

"If you t-t-t-try to get anyone's attention," Hansen hissed at his captive. "I will k-k-k-kill both you and them."

Hansen then bragged that he already had a rock solid alibi. He had convinced a friend to lie for him.

They would drive to Merrill Field airport where he told ominously told her that he was going to "take her out to his cabin."

Cindy laid down on the back seat of the car, her hands cuffed in front of her body but her legs free. The car parked and she watched as Hansen began packing gear into his Piper Super Cub (a small two-seat airplane). Seeing her opportunity, Cindy scooted out of the back seat, opened the driver's side door and sprinted toward the nearest street.

Hansen turned around in time to see Cindy running but luckily for the young woman she made it to the busy street.

Robert Yount slammed on his brakes of his trucks on the rainy road. He opened up the passenger side door and picked up the young woman, immediately taken aback by her disheveled appearance. He drove her to the Mush Inn where Cindy ran inside, telling the clerk to call her boyfriend.

Yount would drive on to work where he called the police himself and told her about the half-naked, handcuffed woman he had dropped off at the Mush Inn.

Anchorage police officers arrived at the Inn but Cindy had disappeared. The clerk told them that she had taken a cab to the Big Timber Motel where her boyfriend stayed.

Police would go to the hotel and find her in room 110 of the motel. She was still handcuffed and alone. She told the police about Hansen, describing him as a wiry, scruffy man. He was tall at six feet but she thought he was non-threatening because he spoke with a stutter. She told of her hours of torture and rape, being hung up by her wrists and taken to the airport. The whole story sounded like something out of a horror movie but the detectives believed Cindy.

She was street smart and scared out of her wits. The police drove her out to the hospital but then Cindy insisted on stopping by the airport.

Cindy was then able to positively identify the same plane that she saw Hansen toss weapons inside of. They also talked to a security guard who obtained the license plate of Hansen's vehicle. With a description and now an address in hand, detectives set out to Hansen's home.

Their suspect would arrive shortly after they staked out his home. Everything about him was exactly as Cindy described. He was wiry, nervous and spoke with a stutter.

As non-threatening as could be.

The inside of his home was also like Cindy as described. A moose head on the wall, trophies and news clippings of his hunting exploits.

A hidden panel in his wall would reveal a large cache of weapons.

All of this was legal, however. There was no evidence that Cindy had been raped. The only evidence was that she had been inside his home.

"I was at my friend's house," Hansen explained. "I was repairing a seat for my airplane then I went to the home of another friend. I left his house then went to the airport and installed the seat."

Hansen would deny Cindy's allegations during his interrogation. He deflected, stating that Cindy was telling them lies because he would not pay her extortion demands.

Hansen had an arrest record but his shy and quiet nature put some doubt in the mind of the cops. Police corroborated his alibi with his friend, John Henning, and the case went cold.

Cindy identified Hansen in a police lineup and insisted that he was the man who raped her. Things went south in the investigation, however, when Cindy refused to take a lie detector test. She had an inherent distrust of police and if they wouldn't take her at her word, she was willing to put the whole thing behind her.

She knew that Hansen was taking her on a one way trip to her death and she escaped. She also knew that the police didn't take prostitutes seriously.

So she walked.

She drifted in and out of the area and couldn't be reached when the police wanted to follow up. The case would be suspended.

But Detective Glenn Flothe of the Alaska State Troopers had already made the determination that the several bodies found around the area was the work of one man.

A serial killer.

And there was something about Robert Hansen that made alarm bells go off. He had a task force go out to the red light districts of Anchorage and warn the women that a serial killer was on the loose.

Then he got the FBI involved.

BRING IN THE BIG GUNS...

Flothe would team up with FBI special agent Roy Hazelwood in developing a psychological profile of the kind of man they were looking for.

Hazelwood believed that the killer was a man who was an experienced hunter but with low self-esteem. He would have a history of problems with women and would keep "souvenirs" of his kills such as a piece of jewelry or article of clothing. Hazelwood also believed that the killer would be socially awkward with a speech impediment.

Flothe used the profile and quickly narrowed down his investigation to Hansen. They would go to Hansen's home and bring him in for investigation. His team would then get a warrant to search Hansen's house, cars, and plane. They would discover jewelry belonging to the missing women as well as a cache of weapons hidden under the insulation in Hansen's attic. They would find the rifle they believed was used to kill two of the topless dancers as well as the revolver with the wooden handle he used to kidnap Cindy Paulson.

The mother lode, however, was an aviation map with little "x" marks all over it, indicating where Hansen had murdered his victims.

The search warrant was being executed at the same time that Hansen was placed into the interrogation room.

Investigators had decorated the room with pictures of his victims, maps of where they found the woman's bodies and crime scene photos.

They wanted to get inside his head, to let him know that they were on to him.

The man who psychologically tortured so many women was now having the script flipped on him.

INTERROGATION AND REVELATION

Another break in the case would come when the neighbor of Hansen noticed the police outside his home. She inquired as to what was going on and was told that Hansen was under investigation for murder. She quickly recanted her husband's story, stating that he had lied to cover up for Hansen and he did not know the extent of his crimes.

Investigators demanded an explanation of why Hansen had possession of the necklaces of the dead women. Hansen would deflect and deny until the interrogators finally cornered him. He would then get defensive, blaming the women and justifying his actions until he finally cracked.

"I started in 1971," Hansen said. "They were usually young. Like sixteen and nineteen. I didn't move to the prostitutes and strippers until later. I would get mad at them sometimes, sure. They would raise their prices on me."

Hansen would be arrested and charged with assault, kidnapping, multiple weapons possession as well as theft and insurance fraud (Hansen had filed a fake claim stating that someone had stolen his trophies. He used the proceeds to buy his private plane.)

Striking a plea bargain, Hansen would participate in telling the police about the markings on his aviation map in order to locate the bodies of his victims. He did this on the condition that they left his family alone and that it would not be publicized. An agreement was reached and Hansen would plead guilty to the murders of Morrow, Messina, Goulding and "Eklutna Annie".

"I began killing in the early 1970s," Hansen said. "Sometimes I would let the girl go. But only if she could convince me that she would not go to the cops."

Hansen would lead police to over seventeen grave sites. He would refuse to give up three marks on his map (two of these are suspected to belong to the spots where he killed Mary Thill and Megan Emrick, both of whom Hansen has denied killing.)

Hansen would be sentenced to 461 years plus life in prison without the possibility of parole. He would later be sent to the Anchorage Correctional Complex for health reasons and would die at the age of 75 on August 21st, 2014.

The identity of "Eklutna Annie" remains unknown.

The Racist Serial Killer

Nancy Meghan White

In Kansas City, Missouri, on August 18, 2017, Fredrick Demond Scott, age 22, was arrested and charged with two counts of first-degree murder and two counts of armed criminal action in the shooting deaths of John Palmer, aged 54, and Steven Gibbons, aged 57— the first and the last victims of the Indian Creek Murders. The Indian Creek Murders consisted of five white, middle-aged men. All were shot from behind and all except the last were shot on the walking and biking trails known as The Indian Creek Trail, thus the name Indian Creek Murders. Although Scott was arrested and charged on August 18, 2017, Jackson County Prosecutor Jean Peters Baker did not officially announce his arrest until August 27, 2017, when it was also announced that Scott was the suspect in the other three murders along the Indian Creek Trail.

These five murders happened over a span of nine months from August 2016 until April 2017 in a killing spree that left Kansas City men afraid to walk along trails alone and took police a year to solve only two of them.

After his arrest, Scott told investigators first that the gun fired accidentally as he pulled it from his pocket. Then police gathered DNA evidence that linked Scott to both the Gibbons and the Palmer murder scene. Scott then admitted to killing both men. Later, in an interview with investigators, Scott mumbled, "they [the victims] never saw it coming."

Scott told police that he was upset over the 2015 shooting death of his half brother, Gerrod Woods, with whom he had a very close relationship.

Gerrod was Scott's half brother by their father Tyrone Scott. However, his mother La'Kesha and her husband, Gerald Woods, Sr who adopted Gerrod, giving him the Woods last name, raised Gerrod.

Fredrick Scott was raised by his mother and has four living siblings, all of whom wish to remain anonymous. Scott's mother has said that Scott began exhibiting symptoms of paranoid schizophrenia at about the age of 16, as did his older brother. Scott, however, refused to get treatment for his condition and it worsened over the years.

On April 7, 2013, Scott's mother called police on him during an argument and in 2014, Scott was in court for assaulting his mother. Scott's mother says she was trying to get him to seek professional help at a mental health clinic for the paranoid schizophrenia. Scott was an adult and she could not force him to go. She did tell him on two occasions that he would have to move out if he did not "get himself together and get help." An argument erupted and Scott shoved her several times. This assault resulted in her calling the police. In January of 2014, while attending his senior year at Center Alternative School in Kansas City, Missouri, Scott found himself in trouble for saying that he wanted to "shoot the school up Columbine-style" and "kill the white people." Scott's mother said he never had any hatred toward white people that she knew about and that he even did odd jobs for a few white men. He received a suspended 180-day sentence for the threat against the Center Alternative School. Public records show that Scott was picked up for shoplifting in 2016.

Despite his troubles, Scott finished his term at Center Alternative School and graduated and received his diploma at the age of 20 after repeating his senior year. "His teachers and his principal were very supportive of him," Scott's mother said. "They really worked with him over there."

Scott worked odd jobs and had a job at a local Burger King in the vicinity of the murders. It is still unclear whether the killings were racially motivated, and some people are asking if one racist statement in the past can make these killings "hate crimes" or not.

People who know Scott said his half brother's murder sent him over the edge.

"He felt like his brother was the only person in the world who loved him," one of his Burger King co-workers told the Star. "It really damaged him."

In December of 2015, Scott's half brother Gerrod Hassan Woods, aged 23, was shot and killed along with another man during a robbery. This is the incident he cited as having him upset when he was arrested for the Gibbons murder. However, a black man killed his half brother, while Scott's victims were white, middle-aged men, most of them walking alone with their dogs. Gibbons was the exception. Video surveillance shows Scott follow Gibbons off a city bus. He then shot Gibbons and proceeded to turn around and get back on another bus. Therefore, Gibbons was shot on a city street whereas the other men were shot on the Indian Creek Trail or very near it.

Later, it was discovered that Scott had reported handguns as being stolen on four separate occasions. When asked if four separate stolen gun reports would not raise some red flags, Kansas City Police Captain, Stacey Graves said the department could not discuss the case against Fredrick Scott because the investigation is ongoing and still open, but she agrees that the stolen gun reports should have "raised some red flags." According to court documents that outline all five killings, the first three happened within days, and even hours, of Scott's stolen gun reports. Concerning the stolen gun reports, Graves also said, "That is something that is being investigated. It will be something we look at." It is still unclear when the fourth gun was reported stolen.

Of all the guns used in the killings, police have recovered only the 9 mm handgun, which, according to court records, Scott told detectives he used to kill Gibbons.

Scott had reported that gun stolen, also. Even though he denied any involvement in three of the killings, Scott told investigators he reported the guns stolen to disassociate himself from the killings.

Mark Jones of Chicago, a retired supervisory special agent in the ATF, said police should follow up immediately when someone reports a second gun theft because the victim is either complicit in the theft or the victim needs to better secure and protect firearms from theft. "I can see where you can report a gun stolen because you know it is going to be used in a crime, but I think you can only get away with that once," Jones said.

Kansas City Police Chief, Rick Smith, said at least 50 law enforcement personnel have worked on the investigation of the killings. The FBI assisted. On Tuesday, Smith said he extended his condolences to the families of the victims.

Police suspect that Fredrick Scott used the guns he reported stolen to commit these crimes and then reported them stolen to throw off investigators.

Brian Darby told The Star that he feels disrespected by the account given by Scott's mother that he suffers from paranoid schizophrenia. He feels the schizophrenia will be used as a defense for Scott.

THE INDIAN CREEK MURDERS:

Five middle-aged white men fatally shot from behind in sneak attack murders in Kansas City, Missouri. All victims were between ages 54 and 67, male, white, all but one were walking their dogs along Indian Creek Trail and in at least two cases, the dogs stayed by their slain owners until police arrived. The profiles of the victims made them relatively rare among Kansas City homicide victims. Some of the men were killed while walking their dogs.

The unsolved killings mystified Kansas City residents and spread fears of a serial killer.

First victim: John Palmer, aged 54, was shot several times, including in the back and his body dragged off the trail into the woods. He was found August 19, 2016 off East Bannister Road and Lydia Avenue in the small wooded area near the Indian Creek Trail. Police found a t-shirt at the scene with DNA that matched Fredrick Scott—who, a year later, under arrest for the Gibbons killing, admitted killing Palmer. Palmer was a man, who relatives said, liked to go on long walks through nature. Palmer's first cousin, Janelle Kristian of Olathe county, said he was, "a man of integrity, honesty and caring."

They grew up in the same household as children according to KANSASCITY.COM.

Second victim: David Lenox, aged 67,was found dead of a gunshot to the back of his head, only a few feet from his front door where he was walking one of his dogs, in the 9900 block of Walnut Street on February 27, 2017. A single .380-caliber shell casing lay close by the body. The police report that Lenox's dog stayed by his body until they arrived.

Third victim: Timothy S. Rice of Excelsior Springs, aged 57, was found dead on April 4, 2017, inside a shelter at Minor Park near East Red Bridge Road and 110th Street. He had been shot multiple times, including in the head. Police found several 9mm shell casings at the scene. Two hours after Rice was found, Scott reported a 9mm handgun stolen.

Hannah Rice, daughter of third victim, Timothy Rice, opened up about her dad and said she wanted the public to know him. "My dad was one of the friendliest people you could ever meet, he didn't know a single stranger," Hannah Rice wrote about her father in an email to The Star Monday evening.

She said in her message that her dad, who had been an electrician most of his life, "could make conversation with anyone at anytime." And, she said that after 13 years of being divorced, her dad and mom had remained friends and had lunch together on the day he died.

"I will always remember how he loved taking me as a child on hikes and fishing trips, we always would compete on who could catch the most fish. My father wasn't perfect by any means but he had a genuine heart," Hannah Rice wrote.

"No one ever expects something like this to happen in your life. To have your loved one brutally taken away from you," she said, adding that her heart goes out to the other four families who also lost loved ones.

Her message thanked Kansas City police for all their hard work on the murders. "They have done a phenomenal job chasing leads and working nonstop to catch this violent person," she said.

Hannah Rice also called for the public to provide police with help in the case.

"I also want to urge anyone to come forth with any information you may have no matter how small," she wrote. "It may just be the right information KCPD needs to see all of our families the justice we deserve."

Fourth victim: Michael Darby, aged 61, was found dead on May 18, 2017 from a single gunshot to the back of the head, along Indian Creek Trail off 103rd Street, about a half-mile east of the popular Coach's Bar & Grill where he was a co-owner. The bar was closed by flooding a month ago and may never reopen. The police found a single .22-caliber shell casing near the crime scene. The victim's son, Brian Darby, wonders if more could have been done to prevent the last deaths, including that of his father.

In June 2017, police released a 29-second surveillance video showing a man walking along Indian Creek—a man who police thought might have vital information about the killing in May of Coach's co-owner, Michal Darby. The Kansas City police asked the public for information on June 27, 2017, stating that the person in the video was not considered a suspect in the homicide.

Scott, after his arrest, admitted that he was the man shown in the surveillance video circulated by the Kansas City police department.

Brian Darby says he feels disrespected by the claims of Scott's mother that her son was suffering from paranoid schizophrenia at the time of the murders.

Scott's mother, added that maybe in jail he'd finally get help: "I don't want those demons in him anymore because a person who has never dealt with paranoid schizophrenia — you don't know what it's like. It's hell. Their life is hell."

A lot of people would just as soon not hear that. First, citing a mental illness is seen as making an excuse, which is seen, by many as an affront to the victims and their loved ones.

After the loss of his father and then his father's business, it is quite easy to understand why he would question the motives of Scott's mother in speaking about her son's mental state. Or why he scoffs at the comment that she "says she's hurting just as much as the families of the victims. My father will never get his morning walk again. He'll never see the sun again. He won't get his three meals a day, which her son still has."

In the middle of a rather hot political argument over whether hate crimes from the left are as much a threat as those from the right, conservatives point to this series of unprovoked killings as proof they are correct.

Then there is the pressure from advocates for those who struggle with mental illness. With the ancient stereotype of "all persons with mental illness pose a threat and are dangerous" They are very eager to acknowledge that while the vast majority of those with mental illness are not dangerous, it is possible that sometimes, some mentally ill people do pose a threat.

It is proven however, that racial animus is an obsession, a symptom that only rears its head after the onset of paranoid schizophrenia. The suspect's mother told The Star that her son refused to get treatment for what she has long seen as his paranoid schizophrenia.

This would definitely be a poor defense for Scott, because "not guilty by reason of insanity" is rarely argued and almost never successful. Congress and half the states passed laws limiting the use of this defense. Now, the legal definition of insanity requires a break from reality that is so severe that the accused no longer knows what he is doing is wrong. This standard goes back to the mid-1800s.

Fifth victim: Steven Gibbons, aged 57, was shot in the back of the head as he walked along a south Kansas City street. Video surveillance shows Scott following him off a bus and down a south Kansas City street on August 13, 2017 and he was later seen running from the scene of Gibbons' murder. Gibbons was found in the 1100 block of East 67th Street and he was rushed to the hospital where he survived on life support for over a day before succumbing to his wounds and dying on August 14, 2017.

SCOTT'S COURT APPEARANCE:

A man suspected in five killing on or near south Kansas City trails has appeared in court, providing the victims' families a first chance to see him in person.

Several relatives dabbed their eyes as they left the courtroom. Afterward, Brian Darby, said, "We want justice." Scott is a suspect in the death of Darby's father, 61-year-old Mike Darby, but hasn't been charged in his killing. The police say, at this time, there is not enough evidence to connect and charge Scott with the other three murders.

The Kansas City Star reports that the court appearance Thursday for 22-year-old Fredrick Scott was brief. Prosecutors received a continuance in the case until Oct. 23 over the objections of Scott's public defender. Prosecutors announced last week that Scott had been charged in two killings and is a suspect in three more over nine months. All five were fatally shot, most from behind.

Police say they aren't sure if the murders were racially motivated, but say the accused told detectives he was upset about the 2015 shooting death of his half-brother. The killer was sentenced last week to 45 years in prison.

"Anyone who shoots innocent people walking on a trail should be prosecuted as heavily as possible," Shaton Duncan, who lives near the trail, told CBS affiliate KCTV.

These horrendous murders terrorized the community for months.

"I was in the Army overseas but I didn't want to walk on the trail by myself, that's how dangerous it felt," area resident Chuck Loomis told the station.

It has been an incredibly difficult six months for the family of David Lenox, but news of an arrest has them feeling more confident than ever they'll see justice for their father.

"Yesterday was very emotional with all the families. It was really hard for everyone," said Mindy Lenox.

Lenox and her brother Mike have lived in a true state of pure heartache for the last six months, endlessly working to keep their father's case in the spotlight.

They say while they didn't know exactly what Jackson County Prosecutor Jean Peters Baker would announce Tuesday, the fact investigators suggested Mindy catch a flight from San Francisco to Kansas City tipped them the news was substantial.

Frederick Scott has been charged with two of the murders along the trail - not with David Lenox's - but he is a suspect.

"Now that we have a name and a picture, anyone that knows Frederick Scott that may not have realized that it was vital information for the police," Lenox said. "If they could come forward, that's what we're looking for so that the remaining three families can receive justice as well."

The family says there is some relief just knowing there has been an arrest and that they can rest easier knowing that justice for David Lenox may only be a few tips away.

"I'm so pleased with the Kansas City Missouri Police Department," Michael Lenox said. "I can't thank them enough. Really just tremendous work on their part. They still got more work to do, but I'm very confident they'll get it done."

Since Tuesday's announcement, there have already been multiple tips called in. And anyone who thinks they might have any information at all is encouraged to call the tip line.

It was the Gibbons killing that led police to Scott, who had been mowing lawns to make money and, during the time of the shootings on the trails, had been working at a Burger King at Red Bridge and Holmes roads — within a few miles of three of the shooting scenes.

According to police in Kansas City, Scott did not own a car during the time of the killings, and got around town much of the time by walking. Also, Scott told investigators that he frequently used the Indian Creek Trail as a shortcut. He had a friend at the Willow Creek apartments near the trail. One of the victims was found shot and killed outside those homes. Other than walking, Scott told police that his primary mode of transportation was the public bus.

Allegedly, the bus is where Scott found Steven Gibbons.

Shortly after noon on Aug. 13, police were called to 1146 E. 67th Street, where officers found Gibbons shot in the back of the head.

Detectives found surveillance video that showed Gibbons, minutes before the shooting, boarding a KCATA bus at 75th Street and Troost Avenue. He was followed by a man carrying an iced tea bottle.

When Gibbons stepped off the bus at 67th Street, the man followed him, walking behind Gibbons closing the distance between them.

The surveillance camera panned away from the scene of the shooting, so detectives did not get a video record of the actual murder, but about 40 seconds later, the video showed the suspect running from the shooting scene and boarding a bus again.

Just west of the crime scene, detectives later found an iced tea bottle like the one in the video.

At a nearby gas station, detectives obtained video showing a man buying a bottle of iced tea just a few minutes before boarding the bus behind Gibbons.

Detectives took a still photo from that video and circulated it among police, who four days after the shooting matched the photo to

Scott, whom they found sitting on a wall and smoking a cigarette at 97th Street and Holmes.

Officers watched Scott throw the cigarette butt on the ground and then picked it up, sending it to the department's Regional Crime Lab for forensic testing. That same day, the lab matched the DNA on the cigarette butt to the iced tea bottle.

When police arrested Scott, he allegedly admitted shooting Gibbons but said it had been an accident – that he had been taking the gun out of his pocket when it went off.

While the motive in the killings remains unclear, Scott repeatedly told investigators that he was angry about the 2015 shooting death of his brother, Gerrod H. Woods, aged 23.

Woods was one of two men fatally shot Dec. 14, 2015 during a robbery near East 73rd Street and Wabash Avenue. On Friday, Jimmie Verge, the man convicted in those killings, was handed a 45-year prison sentence.

CONDOLENCES AND RELIEF FOR FAMILIES AND RESIDENTS

Jean Peters Baker said there was no clear motive in the killings. "To the families, there's no motive that makes sense. There just isn't," she said.

John Palmer's family has endured a difficult year since his death a year ago.

He left behind his wife, two grown children, two grandchildren and a large extended collection of family and friends.

Palmer was found shot several times, including in the back, on Aug. 19, 2016, near the Indian Creek Trail. His body had been dragged off the trail into some woods.

Police found a t-shirt at the scene with DNA that matched Scott — who, a year later, under arrest for the Gibbons killing, admitted killing Palmer, a man who relatives said liked to go on long walks through nature.

"He was walking love," said Janelle Kristian of Olathe, Palmer's first cousin. The two grew up in the same house as children. He was, she said, "a man of integrity, honesty and caring."

Palmer wasn't there for the gathering of some 65 people who always celebrate Thanksgiving together, Kristian said. It's been hard "knowing we won't see him again."

But there was solace, she said, when family members began sharing the news from the prosecutor's office, that someone had been arrested and charged.

"I feel glad to think maybe they have found and stopped who was doing this horrible thing," she said. "It's an awful thing to go through."

Kansas City Police Chief Rick Smith said at least 50 law enforcement personnel have worked on the investigation of the killings. The FBI assisted. On Tuesday, Smith said he extended his condolences to the families of the victims.

"We know this has been an incredibly painful and difficult time for each of you," Smith said. "We have worked diligently to bring the person responsible for these crimes to prosecution."

John Sharp, a former Kansas City council member who now leads the South Kansas City Alliance and was at the press conference Tuesday, said people living near the trails could be relieved to know a suspect has been arrested and charged.

"I think it will bring everybody peace of mind," Sharp said. "We had our south Kansas City Alliance problem-solving event on Saturday and a lady told me that how much she missed walking on the trails but her adult children wouldn't let her walk on them anymore.

"I think she wanted me to reassure her it was safe and of course I couldn't do it," he said. "But now I can."

At this point, everyone involved just hopes to continue to collect more tips and more evidence until they can finally solve the other three murders, whether or not that means convicting Scott of them. Were the killings racially motivated? Were they the result of a paranoid schizophrenic who had no professional help with the disease? Either way, they five victims are still gone, forever. We may never know the whole story behind these horrible events, but hopefully, they will be solved and justice will be served.

SWEDEN'S SERIAL KILLER

ANA BENSON

91

Sometimes the truth is stranger than fiction. This sentence really describes the case of Sture Bergwall, a Swedish man who was once considered the most prolific serial killer in that country. But after another shocking turn of events, he became an example of someone who was completely wronged by the system.

The life of Sture Bergwall is a rollercoaster. He started off as an intelligent young man who had an interest in art and drama even though he lived in a small town. Unfortunately, his addiction to drugs turned him into a criminal. After that, he became known throughout the Europe as Sweden's most dangerous killer after he confessed to thirty cold cases which spanned throughout the decades.

But he did eventually come clean and claimed that every single story he told was a lie. Sture Bergwall, also known as Thomas Quick is now a free man, and his story sounds like something out of a detective novel set in a far corner of Northern Europe.

Early life

Sture Ragnar Bergwall was born on April 26th, 1950 in Korsnäs which is located in Sweden. It is a rural town where nothing interesting happens. He had six siblings, including a twin sister. They were somewhat close, and his sister would later describe him as completely different from the rest of the family. She suspected that he suffered a brain injury while he was at a hospital recovering from tuberculosis. As a matter of fact, he was only seven years old when he contracted the illness and he came back home a year later.

Bergwall was always prone to accidents and another one happened while he was in his early teens. He was playing with his brothers when he stumbled and fell into a gravel pit, hitting his head pretty hard. There was an iron pipe at the bottom of the hole, and Bergwall ran straight into it. The impact was so hard that he felt nauseous right away and started vomiting on the spot. From this moment on he became a different person.

It is hard to say what is true when it comes to Bergwall's childhood, especially if you focus on his initial confessions only. Bergwall himself would say that he grew up in an abusive environment with a father who sexually abused him until he hit puberty and a mother who would beat him on a regular basis. His parents were very religious, and they were a part of the Pentecostal church. Having in mind that Sture Bergwall realized he was a homosexual when he was fourteen, it is clear that his childhood was not easy, especially due to the fact that being queer was not something that was readily acceptable back then.

He clearly stated in his interviews from the 1990s that one of his first memories was when he was only four years old and his father was abusing him. Bergwall's mother walked in the room, saw what was going on, and had a miscarriage right there on the spot. His father showed him the body of his stillborn baby brother who was seven months old and that moment became imprinted forever into Bergwall's mind.

His mother started blaming Bergwall for the miscarriage, so she tried to kill him several times. Winters in Sweden are particularly harsh, and she attempted to drown him in a frozen lake soon after the incident. His mother also tried to push him into traffic. According to initial statements made by Bergwall, the abuse he suffered as a child distorted his views on what is right and what is wrong when it comes to sexuality. So he became interested in younger boys while he was a teenager himself.

His twin sister confirms that she did hear her parents say that Bergwall was indeed abusing fellow schoolmates and that the children welfare was involved in the situation as well. Bergwall did describe the incidents in detail while he was interviewed by the police in the 1990s, and would say that it was called *The Strangulation Game*. He would go to the showers with his classmates, put his arm around one's neck, and touch his genital area with a free hand. Bergwall did not think it would be considered abuse and he saw it as natural curiosity regarding human body since he was only twelve at the time.

According to Bergwall, he met a man who was in his twenties and the two became really close friends. The said man loved to drive around and meet younger boys which did partially explain why he apparently befriended Bergwall. They really liked each other, so the unnamed man invited Bergwall to accompany him on the long drives. Bergwall became the one who would talk to the boys first, inviting them to the man's car where they would be eventually molested. He would take part in the abuse sometimes while the man watched and touched himself. Bergwall was only fourteen years old when this was allegedly happening.

The first murder?

During the time Bergwall spent driving around with the unnamed man, the two of them visited an amusement park. It was a weekend, and the park did have a large number of visitors. Bergwall met a boy who was around his own age. His name was Thomas Blomgren, and they struck a conversation right away. After spending hours and hours wandering around, Bergwall suggested that they should explore the nearby woods. When they reached a fairly secluded place, Bergwall attacked the boy, strangling him to death. His first murder was closely linked to the so-called *Strangulation Game* he had played in school because after he murdered Blomgren with his bare hands, Bergwall proceeded to touch his genitals.

Bergwall left Blomgren's body in the woods and set out to find the man who was his ride back home. Once they were in the car, Bergwall told him what he had done, and the man promised he would never tell on him. This event apparently strengthened the bond they shared. But of course, according to his confessions, this wasn't the end of Bergwall's murderous urges. As a matter of fact, Bergwall found his next victim one year later, but the incident was ruled out as an accidental drowning. Bergwall was hanging out by Lake Åsnen when he saw a thirteen-year old boy Alvar Larsson on the shore. He snuck up to the boy and pushed him into the water. The boy was quickly pulled under, and he drowned. Since there were no witnesses, the authorities were certain that the boy slipped, and fell into the lake. No one had any suspicions about a second person being involved.

The time went by, and according to Bergwall, he was laying low. Recreational drug use became his new hobby, and he was addicted to amphetamines at that time. According to his confessions, he was managing to suppress his homicidal thoughts during this time. He was sent to a rehab facility when his parents found out about the drugs he was taking. Bergwall would say that he befriended and killed a boy who was staying with him in the rehab. These claims were never confirmed by the law enforcement or the staff who worked at the rehab clinic. He was released a couple of months later and was in search of a job. Bergwall ended up working as a medic which supposedly gave him access to potential victims. Even though he was doing his best not to be discovered, Bergwall did try to strangle another boy who was staying at the hospital. He stopped before it was too late and felt terrible afterward.

Bergwall thought that a confession to a priest would relieve his consciousness, so he visited a church soon after this incident. Yes, no one was hurt, but the priest called the police and told them about the attempted murder. They brought him to the police station and did a psychological evaluation which revealed that he was a deeply disturbed individual. He was placed in a psychiatric hospital and Bergwall spent the next three years of his life locked away from the society.

This didn't mean that the people around him were safe because according to his later confessions, the security measures in the psych ward were almost non-existent and he was able to get away with many things, including the murder. Bergwall claimed that he strangled another patient, and the staff did not manage to prevent this. Bergwall also told the authorities that he was free to walk out of the psychiatric hospital whenever he wanted. His story was that the security did not even try to stop him. This is highly unlikely because psychiatric hospitals do have high-security measures.

Getting caught and the series of confessions

Everything will start unraveling in 1990 when Bergwall tried to rob a bank with his 16-years old accomplice. They created a large commotion by taking the bank manager's family as hostages. The duo needed money to buy drugs, so they were ready to do anything. The police intervened, and both of them were arrested. Bergwall ended up in prison that specialized in criminally insane inmates. And this is where he started confessing to his crimes. He also dropped the name Sture Bergwall and decided to call himself Thomas Quick. As you might recall, Thomas was the name of his alleged first victim. Quick was his mother's maiden name.

Bergwall who was now called Quick started attending therapy sessions which were a part of his rehabilitation program. He openly talked to his therapist about the crimes he had committed, and that number slowly grew. The therapist who was in charge contacted the police, and they started interviewing Bergwall after each and every session. The detectives were taking notes, and building a case surrounding Bergwall. Some of his claims seemed almost impossible because he was confessing to so many cold cases which were gathering up dust on police shelves for years. Some of the murders were quite old, and the police were unable to present them during the trials because the statute of limitations has expired.

One thing was immediately strange to the outside critics of the Swedish police, and that was the fact that there wasn't any physical evidence that would link Bergwall to the murders. As a matter of fact, each session was based solely on recovered memory therapy methods which did seem factual back then. However, recent studies did show that this type of treatment is not 100% certain, and some patients create false memories which lead to many inconsistencies. Since

Bergwall was unable to provide all the information about the murders, his therapist stated that his mind buried down the memories because they were simply too much to process.

Bergwall's therapist included benzodiazepines which were supposed to help him clear up his mind and relax. This was a wrong move because the doctors failed to acknowledge Bergwall's history of substance abuse. Some experts would say that there is a possibility that these medications triggered some sort of hallucinations which made Bergwall believe in his fabricated memories. But the truth was completely different, and it would be revealed decades later.

His testimonies were believable to the law enforcement back in the 1990s, and Bergwall quickly became Sweden's most prolific serial killer. The body count of his alleged victims grew after each and every therapy session. It did seem impossible that he knew so many details about unsolved murders, but there were many mistakes which were often disregarded by the interrogators who would continue to feed him information during the post therapy interviews. He could give the general description of a crime, but he was murky about the details. Whenever Bergwall got stuck, he would read the detective's facial expressions and try to come up with an acceptable answer. Some police officers did think that since he had many victims, he was starting to mix them up.

In the end, Bergwall confessed to around thirty murders. They were committed all over Scandinavia which included Sweden, Norway, Denmark, and Finland. It did sound a bit far-fetched, and critics started emerging right away, claiming that the police is abusing a mentally unstable person. One of them was an investigator who worked on a case to which Bergwall confessed. But since Bergwall claimed that he committed the first crime when he was only fourteen years old, the law enforcement apparently believed in his testimonies and proceeded to place Bergwall in front of a judge.

The trials

Sture Bergwall went through a total of six trials, starting in 1994 with the last one held in 2001. The majority of the murders he apparently committed were old, and there was no possibility for him to stand a trial for each and every one of them. Bergwall's defense was led by Claes Borgström, a well-known Swedish lawyer, and politician. He failed to see through Bergwall's false confessions and did a poor job of defending his client.

The first trial focused on the murder of Charles Zelmanovits who disappeared in 1976 in Piteå. The partial remains were found in 1993, but since the body was completely decomposed, the forensic experts were unable to tell exactly what happened to Zelmanovits. The detectives accepted Bergwall's version of the story, and the whole case relied solely on his testimony. He was found guilty without a single proof that he was even there when the murder occurred.

Then there were Marinus and Janni Stegehuis, a couple of Dutch tourists who were visiting Sweden in the summer of 1984. They camped by a lake near Appojaure. The couple wanted privacy, so they set up their tent in a secluded place. Other visitors to the camp site would find their bodies a day later. Both of them were brutally stabbed to death, possibly while they were sleeping. Other campers did see a suspicious looking man on the evening when the murders happened. He was covered in blood which did scare everyone who noticed him walking by the lake.

He was identified and questioned by the police, but claimed that he was a hunter and that the blood came from a deer. Eventually, Bergwall confessed to the killings which derailed the investigation. Once again, the investigators couldn't place Bergwall at the scene of the crime, but he did give them some details which were not released to the public. He was found guilty of the murder of the Stegehuis couple in 1996.

Another sentencing came in 1997, and this time it was for the murder of Yenon Levi who was an Israeli tourist traveling through Scandinavian countries. He was killed in 1988. Bergwall gave the investigators his statements about the murder, but there were too many inconsistencies. He couldn't even recall the right murder weapon. Levi was beaten with a wooden club, but Bergwall insisted that he used an axe. After a couple of tries and suggestions made by the police, he did confirm that he killed Levi with a blunt object. The defense did mention that Bergwall struggled a lot with this confession which should have told the judge that he fabricated the entire story. However, Bergwall was found guilty at the end of the proceedings.

Bergwall was on trial for the disappearance of Therese Johannesen in 1998. She was a nine-years old girl from Norway who vanished in 1988. Bergwall did provide the law enforcement with correct details of the abduction, but it would be later discovered that he managed to get his hands on the articles which covered this mysterious disappearance from a news crew who interviewed him while he was in prison. Bergwall claimed that he abducted the girl and then killed her. The only evidence was a bone fragment which supposedly belonged to Therese Johannesen. It would be revealed that no one took time to test the remains and that there were actually made of wood. Not to forget that there was absolutely no proof that Bergwall was even in Norway in the summer of 1988.

Trine Jensen was killed in Oslo in 1981, while Gry Storvik was murdered in the same city four years later. Bergwall included both of these crimes into his confessions, but there was no evidence that could link him to either of the crimes. As a matter of fact, the semen found on Storvik did not match Bergwall's DNA. This didn't stop the judge to find Bergwall guilty in 2000.

And finally, the last trial was centered on one of the most famous criminal cases in the history of Sweden – the disappearance of Johan Asplund. Even though this was the first murder Bergwall talked about during his therapy sessions, it took the investigators nine years to get enough material that can be presented in front of a judge. They couldn't uncover any actual evidence, but they went to the trial in spite of that.

Asplund disappeared when he was on his way to school in November of 1980. He was eleven years old, and his alleged kidnapping launched a huge investigation. Unfortunately, the law enforcement couldn't find the boy or his remains.

Bergwall told his psychiatrist that he waited in front of Asplund's school and then invited the boy in his vehicle. He drove him to the nearby woods where he sexually assaulted Asplund. Once he realized what he did, Bergwall strangled the boy and cut him into pieces. He hid them near the said woods. Bergwall did provide the police with the location of the buried remains, and they headed out in order to find the missing boy. The officers dug through the whole area but their efforts produced nothing. They still had no proof that Bergwall was telling the truth. But regardless of this, Bergwall was found guilty.

The critics and the doubt

As soon as the media started reporting on Bergwall back in 1993, there were a lot of skeptics who did not believe in his confessions. After all, he claimed that he had murdered somewhere around thirty people, but there were absolutely no witnesses or data that could confirm that he was even present at a scene of a single crime. Having in mind that the alleged murders occurred in several countries, it is hard to believe that there wouldn't be any information about his whereabouts.

The tales of alibies and mismatched DNA started appearing in the news, so more and more people started to realize the fact that Sture Bergwall wasn't the boogeyman, but a person with a serious mental illness who simply confessed to a large number of cold cases. If you might recall, Bergwall claimed that his first murder victim was a boy called Thomas Blomgren. Bergwall's own sister debunked this confession by telling the investigators that her brother couldn't have killed the boy since he was actually at their church with the entire family on the day of the murder. Bergwall's confirmation was held on that particular date.

The family members of the murder victims were not satisfied with the trials because they felt like the real killers were out there somewhere. After all, there wasn't a single piece of evidence that could prove that Bergwall killed anyone. If the police did find DNA samples on a victim, they did not match Bergwall's. Yes, it is strange why that didn't raise any red flags among the leading investigators back in the day, but the weirdest thing is that there were more than ten thousand witnesses who were questioned regarding these cases. None of them ever saw Bergwall. It seemed like he had the ability to simply vanish from a scene of a crime which is highly unlikely.

Forensic experts who had worked with the serial killers gave their opinion on Bergwall and stated that he did not match any murderer they had encountered before. He had no clear modus operandi, and according to his own testimonies, he would kill random victims. Murderers are known to have a certain type, but Bergwall didn't care about age, gender, or physical appearance. As a matter of fact, they could only compare him to Henry Lee Lucas, who was known for his fabricated confessions. It was obvious to everyone except the law enforcement that they made a huge mistake.

Bergwall himself attacked the media and the critics in his article which was published in *Dagens Nyheter*. He refused to give the police any additional information about the murders. This meant that his series of confessions was over. He returned to the public's eye in 2006 when a team of lawyers who were hired by some of the victims' parents asked for a case review from the Swedish Chancellor of Justice. They had proof which showed how the entire investigation was conducted poorly, and that Bergwall was mentally ill. These lawyers were backed up by Leif G. W. Persson, a famous criminologist. He was sure that Sture Bergwall was not a killer but a victim of the judicial system that wanted to close the cold cases regardless of who took the blame.

A large number of people believed that Bergwall was not telling the truth while others couldn't understand that someone would confess to a series of murders they didn't commit. So they continued to see him as a ruthless killer who terrorized Scandinavia over several past decades. But everything will soon change.

The actual truth

Sture Bergwall agreed to do a TV interview in 2008. It was supposed to be used for a documentary which described Bergwall's life, but the producers were intrigued when they realized that Bergwall was telling a whole new story. That video footage was the first step that led Bergwall to freedom. Soon after the cameras stopped rolling, Bergwall hired a new lawyer - Thomas Olsson. Olsson was familiar with the case and was ready to listen to Bergwall.

After everything he had heard regarding the confessions, the medications, and Bergwall's own history of drug abuse, Olsson was completely certain that Bergwall was not a murderer and that he should be set free. He would later say: "He is not dangerous at all! I don't like people too much in general. But, of course, if you spend so much time with a client, you always see the person behind the headlines. It all starts with a little boy under a Christmas tree, playing with toys and it ends up very tragic. Somewhere along the line, everyone is a victim."

Olsson dug deep into the procedures of the cases and did a thorough research even though there were a lot of paperwork that covered each and every trial. He discovered plenty of irregularities and omitted evidence that was not disclosed to all sides. One of the crucial things that were never told to the judge was the usage of benzodiazepines during Bergwall's therapy sessions. This evidence alone was enough to completely throw out each conviction. Bergwall did admit that he made up the stories in order to get more drugs and to be taken seriously in a facility where he was being kept back then.

Sture Bergwall asked the Svea Court of Appeal to grant him a new trial for the murder of Yenon Levi, and once it was approved, the ball started rolling. The new trial was scheduled for the winter of 2009.

Olsson told the new judge about the interview with the police and the fact that his client did not know the exact murder weapon. As a matter of fact, he was coerced or led to the correct answer by the police officers who were present in the interrogation room. Bergwall was cleared of any suspicion, and judge's initial ruling was thrown out.

The next step was the case of Therese Johannesen. Bergwall's new lawyer had enough proof to claim that his client had an alibi for the day of the disappearance. The charges were dropped soon after. Olsson did plan to appeal to every single conviction, but the prosecution knew that the entire case was falling apart. Sture Bergwall was cleared of all charges in 2013. He left the Säter's institution for the criminally insane under the condition that he attends therapy.

Bergwall passed his psychological examination after the release, and it showed that there was no need for him to continue to use his medication. The case of Sture Bergwall is a proof how an innocent man can be accused of heinous crimes because the system wants to believe in his guilt. There were plenty of opportunities to put an end to the madness, but the police did nothing. This man did spend a large portion of his life behind the bars, and he will never get that time back. But he did receive the justice he deserved, and hopefully, those cold cases he confessed to will be solved as well.

Football Player & Serial Killer : The True Story of Randall Woodfield

Sarah Teague

On October 9th, 1980, Portland, Oregon police arrived at grime scene. A pretty young woman with soft facial features and dark brown, shoulder-length hair was found dead. She suffered from repeated stab wounds in her neck, as well as evidence of blunt force trauma, as if from a severe bludgeoning. The victim was Cherie Ayers, a twenty-nine year old woman who was found dead in her home. She was the first of a trail of bodies scattered throughout Oregon. From October 1980 to the blistery winter of February 1981, a span of grisly murders would plague the rainy pacific northwest state of Oregon up and down the I-5 - or, the Highway of Hell. The culprit was dubbed "The I-5 Killer", leaving behind at least ten known victims. The identity of the killer turned out to be former 17th round draft pick for the Green Bay Packers, Randall Woodfield.

Randall Woodfield would be convicted of only one of his heinous murders by the summer of 1981, though Woodfield has been tried to at least eighteen victims up and town Interstate 5. Woodfield spent the two years between 1979 and 1981 terrorizing the citizens of Oregon and Washington, a time of horror that lives on in the memories of those that witnessed and lived through it. Woodfield was not born and raised in typical, serial killer fashion. There are no horrors in his past, nor is there a trail of neglect leading back to his childhood. The story of Randall Woodfield turning from Green Bay Packers prospect to serial killer is one that doesn't have a logical explanation.

Just after Christmas Day in December of 1950, Randall Brent Woodfield was born. Woodfield was born into a middle class family in the town of Salem, Oregon. His childhood and homelife were, overall, normal. His family had no dysfunctional habits to speak of. He was the only son of a stay at home mother and a father who worked as the executive of Pacific Northwest Bell, a phone company. Woodfield was his parent's only boy, and no doubt luxuriated in such a fact. He had two older sisters, one of whom worked as a doctor and the other as a lawyer. He grew up middle class with what one would assume would be a fairly comfortable life. The Woodfield family was well-known throughout their community, and had no prior issues with deviant behavior or dysfunction. Growing up, he was a popular kid among the rest of his high school classmates. As well as socially, Woodfield excelled academically. He got good grades, and the teachers had no reason to be concerned with his performance.

It was in highschool that he his natural skills in regards to football were discovered. His parents encouraged him to pursue athletics. With enough talent, Woodfield was the start player of the football team that he played for at Newport High School. Despite his otherwise normal upbringing, and Woodfield's likeability among his peers, teachers and coaches, problems began to arise for Woodfield beginning in his adolescence. He began exposing himself and engaging in otherwise sexually charged antisocial behavior. He got caught exposing himself to women and girls while standing on a bridge. That was his first offense in a long line of criminal behavior that would turn out to shock the entirety of the Pacific Northwest.

There was no outcry from his teachers or coaches, however. Woodfield was referred, by his parents, to a therapist to talk about the issue. The therapist didn't find any cause for concern, and said that Woodfield was simply a teenager exploring his newfound sexuality. There was such little worry over the incident that Woodfield's coaches managed to get him out of his first arrest during high school, in regards to indecent exposure, so that he could continue his role on the football team. At eighteen, his record was expunged and the first signs of deviant behavior were erased, but for the memories that live on in those that had witnessed it.

Woodfield lived a mostly normal and undisruptive childhood and adolescence. At the least, there was nothing to suggest the dangerous and dark path he would soon head down that would lead police slogging through victims up and down the I-5 through Oregon and Washington. From Newport High School's team, Woodfield went on to Portland State University, where he continued to play football - and where his behavior continued to take a turn for the worst. Despite this, many people had only good things to say about Woodfield.

Woodfield was recalled differently between both his teammates and his coaches at Portland State University. Gary Hamblet, who worked as a PSU receivers coach during the time that Woodfield attended college there, recalls him to have been "the nicest, most gentlemanly kid" he ever knew. On the other hand, a former PSU teammate said this of Woodfield: "You just had a bad feeling about the guy, like there was something underneath his mask."

Woodfield, despite playing on the football team, was hesitant to allow himself any physical contact with the other players. He was incredibly fast, and his coaches remarked on his speed that made him a valuable player. It was just that Woodfield had an aversion to allowing himself to be hit by anyone else on either his own or the opposing the team.

This aversion was just part of Woodfields general personality. He was soft spoken and would avoid confrontation, which made him well liked by teachers and coaches. Woodfield was also considered quite handsome, standing at six feet and muscular, with dark hair and a distinguished mustache that wouldn't be out of place for a college-aged guy in the 70s. His general attractive demeanor made him just as likeable as his personality.

Woodfield took part in the Campus Crusade for Christ, as well as the Fellowship of Christian Athletes. He was well known for both of these activities, and his teammates recall them being a very important part of his life at Portland State University. Woodfield would have been considered a "good guy", as demonstrated by his devotion to the on-campus Christian organizations. This gentle demeanor, however, was at severe odds with the criminal and antisocial behavior that Woodfield often demonstrated. Woodfield was 20 years old when, in 1970, he was arrested for the vandalization of an ex-girlfriend's apartment in Ontario, Oregon while he was attending a community college before his eventual transfer to Portland State University. He was arrested twice more that year for displays of public indecency. The amicable quality about him that Woodfield had demonstrated during his time at Newport High School didn't seem to follow him to PSU.

Woodfield's teammates had a mixed bag of feelings towards him. He was described by one of his teammates, Jon Carey, as "confident in himself, but not to the point of being cocky". He wasn't a loner by any means, and had a relatively normal dating history. Despite this, some of Woodfield's other teammates remember him being a little strange. According to some, Woodfield was prone to making statements that seemed apropos of nothing, with his line of thinking hard to follow.

While he was attending PSU, Woodfield was being watched by scouts for the Green Bay Packers. Strangely enough, no one thought to run any sort of background check. In the 17th round of the NHL draft picks that year in 1974, Green Bay drafted Randall Woodfield, unknowing of both his previous foray into antisocial sexual behaviors or the arrests on his record for indecent exposure and vandalism. Perhaps, had they known, the Packers would not have continued on with Woodfield on their team. Woodfield did not hesitate once offered the contract. He was on the edge of making it big, having been signed to play in the NFL. He was given a $16,000 one-year contract with thousands of dollars in bonuses if he played well.

However, Woodfield stay with Green Bay would be short lived. He attended a training camp during April of 1974 located in Scottsdale, Arizona. He was assessed by the coaches and seemed to have high hopes of cutting it on the team. In July, Woodfield competed in a game against the Bears which turned out as well as expected. Woodfield continued to make several cuts, and was otherwise looking forward to staying on with the Packers and the NFL. In August of 1974, however, Woodfield was abruptly cut from the team. He stayed in Wisconsin after this, and played for the Manitowoc Chiefs in hopes that the

Packers would change their mind and welcome him back onto the team.

Woodfield played well, and got along with his teammates in Manitowoc. He continued having a relatively well-rounded life, with teammates, friends and girlfriends. After his first season with Manitowoc, though, Woodfield was let go from that team as well. It was shortly after his release from the Chiefs that Woodfield drove back to his home state of Oregon. It was that year in 1975 that Woodfield escalated from petty vandalism and indecent exposure to crimes that would become more and more horrific as time went on.

Woodfield's crime spree began in the early months of 1975. In Portland, a string of women were being held at knife-point by a man who would then rape them or force them to perform sexual acts on him. The man would then rob them of their handbags, though murder did not seem to be on the agenda for this particular assailant. Portland police used female police officers as undercover decoys to catch the perpetrator, and used marked dollar bills to track down the man. As it turns out, it was Randall Woodfield. In early March, Woodfield was arrested after trying to rob the undercover female officers. In April that same year, Woodfield plead guilty to second-degree robbery. He was originally sentenced for ten years in prison, but managed to get out on parole in July of 1979.

There's no way to tell what happened in those four years that Woodfield spent in prison. There is also no way to tell if he had served out his full span of ten years, whether or not he would have eventually escalated his crimes the way that he did. All that is know, is that after his released from prison in July of 1979, Woodfield began his reign of terror enacted along the I-5 that lends him his nickname, the I-5 Killer.

Woodfield's first known victim was 29 year old Cherie Ayers, though there's no way to tell if Woodfield was simply not able to be connected with any previous murders before October 8th in 1980. Ayers was one of Woodfield's former classmates at Newport High

School. They knew one another casually, socially, after they had reconnected at their high school reunion. She was found dead in her apartment in Portland. She was beaten to death and stabbed in her throat. There was also evidence of sexual assault to her body. Woodfield was picked up for this crime before his spree of killings along the I-5 began. Unfortunately, police were unable to link him to Cherie Ayers, neither by blood test nor semen found on the body. Ultimately, Woodfield was released, despite the police finding him "evasive" when asking questions regarding his possible involvement with the crime.

There's no telling what evading the police made Woodfield feel, or whether or not that incident made him confident enough to continue on with his future murders. On thanksgiving morning, not one month later from Cherie Ayer's death, 22 year old Darcey Renee Fix and 24 year old Douglas Keith Altig were found shot, execution style, in Fix's home in Northern Portland. The gun used was a .32 revolver belonging to fix, which was missing from the crime scene. Sure enough, Woodfield was not a stranger to these two victims, either. Darcey Fix was the ex-girlfriend of one of his former PSU teammates. Police picked up Woodfield a second time, and a second time they were unable to tie Woodfield definitely to the crime.

Throughout December of 1980, Portland was once more plagued with a series of robberies at both knifepoint and gun-point. The assailant as described to be wearing a fake beard and a strip of white athletic tape over his nose, like the kind an athlete would wear. Or, more specifically, the manner in which a football player might wear it. The crimes ranged from armed robbery of a gas station in Vancouver, Washington to forcing a twenty-five year old waitress to masurbate him at gunpoint in the bathroom of a diner. All of these crimes were taking place up and down Interstate 5 that runs up and down alongside the pacific coast between Canada and Mexico. The crimes, however, were isolated to Oregon and Washington, and all happened within two miles of the I-5. This is what lead police to give him the moniker: The

I-5 Bandit, which would later become the I-5 Killer after Woodfield stint with robbery was up and he, once more, turned to murder.

The armed robberies continued on as December turned into a blistery and rainy January of 1981. Throughout January, Woodfield—who was still evading the police, and who was now only known by law enforcement as the I-5 Bandit—would go back and rob the same exact Vancouver gas station, then move on to perform another armed robbery on a market in Eugene. By January 12th, he was in Sutherlin, Oregon, where he wounded a female grocery clerk by gunshot during a robbery of the store. Nowhere was safe. The I-5 Bandit was moving quickly between towns up and down Interstate 5, slipping from Washington to Oregon and leaving no trace of himself behind at his crime scenes.

The crimes kept escalating, going from robbery and sexual assault to pedophilia. On January 14th, Woodfield, wearing his fake beard, committed a home invasion where two young girls lived. They were ages eight and ten. Woodfield force the young children to take off their clothes, then proceeded to sexually assault them. It was only four days later that Woodfield, have returned to his hometown of Salem, Oregon, entered an office building where he once more committed sexual violence against two women by the names of Shari Hull and Lisa Garcia. It was here that Woodfield's life of crime escalated from robbery and rape, once more to murder. Woodfield shot both Hull and Garcia. Hull was killed, while Garcia managed to survive by lying still and pretending to be dead. Throughout the rest of January, Woodfield committed several more robberies and assaults as he moved towards southern Oregon, still using Interstate 5 as his main means of travel, leaving behind a trail of crimes in his wake.

Woodfield escalated to murder once more in February of 1981. This time, Woodfield would have traveled from Oregon into California, causing his crime spree to be spread over three different states. It was on February 3rd that the bodies of 37 year old Donna

Eckard and her 14 year old daughter, Jannell Jarvis, were found in their home in Mountain Gate, California. The crime was gruesome. Mother and daughter were shot multiple times in the head. It was only later revealed, after tests had been conducted on the bodies, that 14 year old Jannell had been sodomized before her death.

The rape and murders of Eckard and Jarvis were not the only crimes that Woodfield allegedly committed that day. Police discovered that earlier in the day on February 3rd, only 15 miles away in Redding, California, a female clerk in a store had been kidnapped during an armed robbery. She had also been raped and sodomized during the event. The crimes were so similar, it was clear the whoever had committed the crimes against Eckard and her daughter had also committed the rape of the young store clerk during the robbery. On February 4th, in Yreka, California, which was 100 miles away from the incidents committed the day before, a man was reported to have raped and sodomized another woman during a robbery. On the evening of the 4th, the same man robbed a motel in Ashland, Oregon.

The crime spree up and down the I-5 was becoming a nightmare. The I-5 Bandit was causing trauma and mayhem wherever he went, with hundreds of miles stretched between each incident, making it almost impossible for law enforcement to tell where he would strike next. The only thing anyone knew was that it would be along the I-5, but with 1,400 miles of ribbon stretched between Canada and Mexico, that could have been anywhere. Women were being told that they needed to be careful, but there was no place to pinpoint where and who was at risk. Woodfield did not seem to discriminate in his targets, other than that they were female: from an eight year old girl to a late-thirties woman, no female seemed to be safe if they were in the wrong place at the wrong time.

February 14th, 1981, an eighteen year old girl by the name of Julie Reitz was shot and killed inside the home of her and her mother, Candee Wilson. Julie was no stranger to Woodfield. He had once let her into a club when she didn't have a legitimate ID. Reitz would mark the third victim of the I-5 Killer that could be directly tied back to Woodfield. The murder of Julie Reitz took place in Beaverton, Oregon, miles and miles away from the last attacks in California. Woodfield was using the I-5 to terrorize everyone, everywhere, seemingly able to disappear from one town and popup in the next in the blink of an eye.

Despite evading law enforcement during the early stages of their investigation into the deaths of Cherie Ayers, Darcey Fix and Douglas Atlig, Randall Woodfield was a prime suspect by police investigators into the many crimes of the I-5 Bandit - and now, too, the I-5 Killer. Woodfield was easily connected to the crimes by police due to the fact that he was connected with several of the victims, and the victims of the crimes that were not connected to Woodfield, personally, still demonstrated the I-5 Killer's M.O. While the investigation turned to Woodfield, the I-5 killer was able to strike several more times before law enforcement were able to get a lead on him. Between February 15th and February 28th, Woodfield managed two more robberies and sexual assaults. Even after having the suspicion and full-focus of police investigators into his crimes, Woodfield was still a terror along the Interstate, wrecking havoc with no foreseeable way to stop him.

Finally, law enforcement got the help they needed. Lisa Garcia, the woman that Woodfield had accidentally left for dead during his attached on Garcia and Sheri Hull, played an instrumental part helping law enforcement finally bring Woodfield down. She worked with the lead investigator on the case, David Kominek, who worked tirelessly and who had already considered Randall Woodfield a suspect back from the Hull murder.

Garcia picked Woodfield out from a line up as the man who had come into her offer and shot and murdered in co-worker, and left her wounded and thought dead. It was this, along with paycard record showing Woodfield making calls up and down the I-5 within miles of where the crime scenes were located, that allowed police to finally make the move to bring Woodfield in for an interrogation.

On March 5th, 1981, Randall Woodfield was brought in for interrogation while police searched his home. Woodfield happened to be staying in a room he was renting from a family in Springfield, Oregon, who had no idea of what their tenant was up to. In his room, police discovered the same brand of tape that had been used to bind some of the victims, as well as a .32 bullet—the same gun used and missing from the Fix murder. The evidence mounted quickly against him, and Woodfield was charged on March 9th, 1981 with the murder of Shari Hull, the attempted murder of Lisa Garcia, and two counts of sodomy. Perhaps it is of little surprise what Woodfield, along with his public defender, plead not guilty to the charges.

From Washington to Oregon, indictments began coming in with charges like: rape, murder, sodomy, attempted kidnapping and armed robbery. In the summer of 1981, the I-5 Killer finally stood trial for all of his crimes in his hometown of Salem, Oregon. Woodfield's not guilty defense hinged on a case of mistaken identity, despite the surmounting evidence against him. The prosecutor of the case described Woodfield as "an arrogant, cold, unemotional individual". The author of the book *The I-5 Killer*, Ann Rule, who spent years covering this case, described Woodfield as "humbled". She said, "He looked, if anything, humbled—a predatory creature brought down and caged in mid-rampage." When it was Woodfield's turn to take the stand, Rule describes him a being incredibly soft spoken. He was still handsome at 30 years old, looking much like he had during his football star glory days.

While Woodfield is handsome, quiet, polite and charismatic, one thing is also clear: he holds no responsibility for his actions, and has no accountability to himself for the crimes he committed. He shows no remorse for what he's done. The evidence against him was enough to counterbalance the soft-spoken personality that Woodfield exhibited in court.

The jury came back in short time. The verdict was in. On June 26th in 1981, Randall Woodfield was found guilty on all four counts: murder, attempted murder, and two counts of sodomy. Oregon does not have the death penalty, and so Woodfield was sentenced to life in prison with an additional 90 years. Unlike Woodfield's first stint in prison, where his ten years was cut short and the would-be killer was released onto the unsuspecting victims he would later enact horrific cruelties on, this sentence was final. Woodfield would not be released again.

After his conviction, other jurisdictions up and down the Interstate 5 would have to decided whether or not they wanted to pursue charging Woodfield with additional crimes. After taking into account the state costs, and the fact that Woodfield would not live to see the end of his sentence, nor would he ever be released from prison, it was decided not to charge Woodfield with the additional counts of murder, rape and robbery that he committed while driving up and down the I-5.

Despite his conviction, and despite other jurisdictions deciding to forgo charging him with any more crimes, Woodfield's crimes continued to add up throughout the years following the trial. With the help of DNA testing, Woodfield was linked to the murders of Darcey Fix, Douglas Altig, Donna Eckard and her daughter Jannell Jarvis, and Julie Reitz. Altogether, despite having no link to the crimes, Woodfield is still suspected of up to 44 homicides with similar M.O's to the I-5 Killer's trail of crimes and victims.

At the age of 66, Woodfield is now living out the rest of his life only a mile away from Interstate 5. He serving out his life sentence and consecutive additional 90 years at the Oregon State Penitentiary in his hometown of Salem, Oregon. While imprisoned, he has been married three times, two of which had ended in divorce.

In 2005, a former police lieutenant went to visit Woodfield in prison in an attempt to garner a confession of related crimes. The lieutenant described Woodfield as charismatic, saying, "He was very charismatic, which makes sense because he would lure victims and get them to let their guard down." However, Woodfield would not confess to any crimes, and was known to stop talking whenever the subject would turn away from anything but football and sports. In 2006, Woodfield signed up for a Myspace page where he admitted to one murder and "many other crimes". Altogether, however, Woodfield does not admit to his slew of heinous crimes that had, for two long years, plagued the residences of Washington to California with fear.

THE WORST SERIAL KILLER IN HISTORY

AMY DELANEY

Robert William Pickton

Robert William Pickton was born in Port Coquitlam, British Columbia, Canada, on October 24th, 1949 to Leonard and Louise Pickton. He was the middle child of three – his sister, Linda, was born a year earlier, and his brother, David, followed a year later, in 1950.

His father, Leonard, was born in England in 1896, but when he was three his family emigrated to Canada. Leonard was perceived as being lazy, and no one held out much hope of him making anything of his life until he astonished everybody by marrying Louise – a woman who was sixteen years younger than Leonard.

Louise was the antithesis of Leonard. Whereas he was lazy, she was a hard worker, and it was she who ran the family's inherited farming business, and also the family.

But Louise was a strange woman. Her physical appearance alone was enough to make her stand out, for all the wrong reasons. While she certainly worked hard at the business, she neglected her appearance dreadfully – as the years progressed she lost most of her hair, and her teeth slowly rotted away. While her head hair became ever scarcer, her facial hair grew in abundance, until she had what could pass as a decent goatee beard on her chin.

Louise's appearance both repulsed and fascinated the locals. She would screech at her children in a high pitched tone and was always seen wearing a housecoat over men's jeans, which were invariably tucked inside men's gumboots.

Leonard's appearance was not dissimilar to his wife's. His clothes were always dirty, and he wore old t-shirts over old jeans, sporting the same heavy gumboots as his wife. However, where Louise was short and fat, Leonard was tall and wiry.

Linda and David took after their mother in appearance, but Robert, or Willie as he was known, was tall and thin like his father, and often described as 'rat-faced' by the locals.

"Piggy"

The strange appearance of the Picktons was nothing compared to their personal hygiene, or lack of it. Leonard was known by his fellow farmers as 'Piggy', and it didn't just refer to the animals who were the main basis of the farm.

Originally, the Pickton's farm was situated on Dawes Hill, but they later moved a short distance to Dominion Avenue. Either way, the farm – and its inhabitants – stank. Louise was oblivious to dirt, and the animals from the farm, such as the many pigs who lived there, as well as ducks, and even cows, were allowed to wander in and out of the family home at will, leaving animal droppings in their wake.

The Pickton children were made to clean out the farm's 200 or so pigs every day before school and would carry the stench with them to lessons. Louise only saw fit to make the children bathe once a week, or even less, but the smell of the farm was deeply ingrained into them and the meagre amount of washing they were made to do did nothing to shift the odour. Whereas Leonard had no problem being called 'Piggy' when the Pickton boys were given the same nickname it hurt.

Linda was spared some of the unhappiness. Louise would send her daughter to birthday parties dressed in pretty clothes and enrolled her in Sunday school. Her sons, however, had to fend for themselves, having little social interaction with other children and were largely left to their own devices on and around the farm in the limited free time they had.

School

Willie started school just short of his sixth birthday, but only a month in he changed schools, from Millside to Viscount Alexander. School records showed that his education test results were far below par.

In the 2nd grade, Willie's teacher kept him back and made him repeat the year as his results, although slightly improved, were still far short of the mark. As humiliating as that might have been for the little boy, it helped, and by the end of his second run of 2nd grade, his results were average.

The school should shoulder some of the blame for his poor education because of their inability to take into consideration the special needs of children who came from rural life – neither of Willie's parents ever read to him, nor encouraged him in literacy or numeracy, or indeed any other area of learning.

By fall of 1955, as Willie was about to enter grade 3, his teachers made the decision to place him in a class for slow learners – in fact, he would stay in 'Special Needs' for the duration of his school life.

However, even with the extra help provided for Willie, school life was miserable. Along with David and Linda, most of Willie's peers were the sons and daughters of affluent professionals such as doctors. Indeed, not only were they their classmates, but also their neighbors, and the 'proper' kids wanted nothing to do with the Pickton children.

Most of them came from the grand houses which stood further up the hill – the homes of the doctors who worked at the sprawling Essondale mental hospital which stood close to the Pickton's farm. At the bottom of the hill, there were more farms, which meant more farm children, but these kids were far feistier than the Picktons and would pick fights with the doctor's children on the school bus. David, Willie, and Linda were in the middle, not affiliated with either type of peer, which just made them stand out even more.

To make matters worse, both the Pickton boys had speech problems, afflictions which didn't go unnoticed by their wealthier counterparts. Both boys talked in a high-pitched voice and spoke quickly. David couldn't pronounce his 'R's, and Willie was withdrawn and didn't speak much at all.

One of these affluent neighbors, a doctor's daughter, recalls:

"We were all terrible to the Picktons, especially Robert [Willie]. I remember all of us on the road taunting him. We'd say to each other 'Just let us at him now and we'll make him talk.' How were they different?

Dirty and Stinky. They always had their hair cut in a brush cut. Man, they stunk. Their house was a poor house with no yard and falling-down fences. There were no big trees, only some shrubs. I don't even remember them at school at all but I do remember them waiting for the school bus. Our bunch was mostly all doctors' kids. We were the best dressed and had the nicest houses; almost everyone in the group is successful now."

The last straw came for Willie when he was 14. He had bought a pen which, when turned upside down, displayed a rude image of a woman. The school principal got wind of the pen and warned Willie that he would beat him. Willie told him that if he did he would walk out of school. The principal stood firm, so Willie left school for good.

Willie's Calf

Willie Pickton had his heart broken at the age of 12. He had saved hard, and when he had enough money, he bought a three and a half week old calf for $35. He loved the calf, and wanted to raise it as a pet, and would tell everyone that he would keep the calf forever. In truth, the calf was probably his only friend, and he loved it. The highlight of his day was coming home to his calf and feeding it. One day, however, when he went to look for his calf and couldn't find it, his mother told him the calf must have escaped, but Willie wouldn't accept that as a plausible answer. Eventually, either Louise or Leonard told him to go and look in the barn.

There he found his calf, hanging and butchered.

Willie was inconsolable. Louise offered him $20 to buy another one, but her son was heartbroken.

"I couldn't talk to anybody for three or four days. I locked everybody out of my own mind, I didn't want to talk to anybody."

The Move

1963 saw the Picktons move their business from Dawes Hill to Dominion Avenue. Linda saw this as an opportunity to get away – she had never been happy with her family, so when the family moved she went to stay with extended family in a nice area of Vancouver, close to the University. Ties to her family back home in Coquitlam were all but severed.

The new farm was situated on 40 acres of land. The old farmhouse from Dawes Hill was lifted and moved to 993 Dominion Avenue, so their housing situation remained the same. The business was, however, expanding. In those days not many people had large freezers in which to keep big cuts of meat, so the Picktons bought a number of industrial sized freezers and set up a business which locals referred to as 'The Meat Locker' – a store where they kept meat which had been purchased by customers who didn't have the room to keep it at home.

By that time the Picktons' farm was home to around 700 pigs, which were once again allowed to wander in and out of the family home. Pretty soon the farmhouse and its surroundings were as disgusting as the previous one.

With Linda gone the work fell to the two boys who were expected to slop out the pigs four times a day – once before school, once at lunchtime when they would have to return home to work, after school, and again before bed. Their attendance at school began to drop under such a heavy workload, and with no shower at the farmhouse, the boys were permanently smelly and filthy. The few baths they did take, as before did nothing to eradicate the stench.

Of course, by the time the family moved to Dominion Avenue, Leonard Pickton was an old man of 77. Although he was there he never really played any part in the children's upbringing, and what little input he did have appeared to be abusive. Stories circulated that Leonard was very cruel to the children, and in particular to Willie. Louise never intervened, according to neighbors, so the abuse went unchecked.

With Willie's school career at an end, Louise had her son's help full-time at the farm. When Louise wanted him to learn how to slaughter the pigs, Willie was reluctant, but nonetheless, he embarked on an apprenticeship as a meat-cutter.

Dave Pickton

In 1967 Dave Pickton had passed his driving test, and on October 17th he took one of his father's trucks and went for a drive. However, as he was driving he hit a 14-year-old boy named Timothy Barrett. Tim had been to visit a friend, but the friend was busy and Tim was walking home when Dave Pickton struck him with the truck. When he saw the young boy's body lying in the road, Pickton drove home in a panic and told Louise what had happened. When she and Leonard saw the damage to the truck, along with blood, they ordered Dave to take the truck to a garage and have the dent knocked out and painted over. In the meantime, Louise went to look for Tim.

When she found him lying beside the road, instead of picking him up and taking him for medical attention, she dragged him the ten yards to the edge of the ditch and rolled him in, before returning to the farm.

Dave had taken the car to the Pickton's mechanic as instructed. The mechanic could clearly see the damage – there was a bowl-shaped dent in the fender and hood, and the light socket for the turn signal had been torn out. The shape of the damage didn't sit well with the mechanic when Dave told him some timber had fallen on the truck – it just didn't match his account of what had happened.

The mechanic obliged by mending the dent and fixing the light. But he refused to paint over the damage – the Picktons' trucks were beat-up wrecks most of the time, and he could see no point in covering up that damage when the truck was riddled with others.

While Dave was getting the truck fixed, Tim Barrett's family were becoming concerned. By 11 pm Mr Barrett called Tim's friend, whose father explained that Tim had left early that evening. A search party went out looking for the boy and in the early hours of the morning, they stumbled upon Tim's shoe lying at the side of the road. Tim's distraught father was part of the search party, and he walked to the ditch and looked in, seeing his 14-year-old son lying dead in the water.

The following morning, the mechanic was listening to the news when he heard about Tim. Recalling Dave Pickton's visit the night before, he called the police and told them what had transpired. With a search warrant, the police examined the truck and samples of paint from the dent matched paint found on Tim's body. Pickton was placed on probation and had his licence revoked until he reached the age of 21.

The coroner's report showed that Tim had not died of his injuries, but that he had drowned in the ditch – Louise Pickton had been the one to cause his death, although she was never implicated in the case.

Willie Pickton had just had his first lesson in getting away with murder.

Things Change

On New Year's Day 1978 Leonard Pickton died. He had been sick for a number of years with dementia, and shortly before his death, he had been diagnosed with cancer. Dave had moved his girlfriend, Sandy, into the farmhouse and the couple had two children, but by the time Leonard died the couple weren't happy, and Sandy moved out, taking the two children with her. Willie was devastated – far more than Dave was – as he was very fond of Sandy and the children, so much so that he had, at one point, asked Sandy to marry him.

The same year six hundred of the farm's pigs were lost when a fire tore through the place, destroying the barns.

That year's events were traumatic enough, but the following year even more tragedy struck when Louise also died from cancer. Willie had been close to his mother and was once again devastated by the loss. He had nursed her through her final weeks, and he felt her death keenly.

Dave, on the other hand, was more resilient, both over the loss of his parents, and his girlfriend. In fact, it didn't take him long to move a new girlfriend into the farmhouse.

Dave's new love interest, Vicky Evans, had two younger sisters called Samantha and Alison, who would regularly visit the farm. Willie was kind to the girls and allowed them to ride on the horses. Alison was six when she first visited the farm, and Samantha was 14.

Dave, by this time, had started his own business, moving and delivering topsoil, and Willie had thrown in the towel on his butchery apprenticeship. The farm was slowly going to wrack and ruin as Dave filtered off the top soil from the farm, and Willie bought old wrecks and parked them in the grounds. The farm was now owned by the three Pickton siblings, but Willie's share was carefully controlled by Dave and Linda, whom Louise had left in charge. While his brother and sister had instant access to their money, Louise stipulated in her will that Willie would not get his money until he was 40 years old, providing he stayed on the farm until that time. The only caveat to that was that Willie would receive a $20,000 lump sum up front to keep him going. He was incensed – Linda was doing well, and Dave had his business, but Willie was tied to the farm until he was 40.

He was angry.

Hell's Angels

Word reached the local police that the Pickton's were running an illegal 'chop shop' with the local Hell's Angels and that they were using the farm as a base for taking apart stolen vehicles and selling the parts.

Dave had expanded his business into demolition and was too busy to help Willie, so it was down to him to run the bikers' business. At the same time he was also trying to run the pig business, so he began to employ young men to help out. The bikers would intimidate the young lads and send them off to steal cars for them. The youngsters didn't mind – at least they got paid for it, unlike the jobs they did for Willie who would promise them payment and then not follow through.

Although the police investigated, nothing was done. As far as they were concerned the Picktons and the Hell's Angels were running nothing more serious than a car theft racket and turned a blind eye to it.

But the brothers continued to cause problems. Dave ran up a slew of driving violations, but nothing phased him or Willie. In 1992, though, Dave was charged with sexual assault against a girl who was working on a project for him, after gaining access to her trailer. But the Hell's Angels had his back, and the girl began receiving threats. In the end, Dave Pickton received a paltry fine and a telling off. His relationships started and ended, and as soon as one would finish another would start. He had a dreadful reputation for abusing women, but it never stopped him having a queue of women lining up to be his next girlfriend.[1]

Stitch

On Saturday, March 22nd, 1997, a 31-year-old prostitute and mother of two was picked up by Willie in his truck in Vancouver's Downtown Eastside. He had become a regular there, picking up prostitutes and drinking in seedy bars. Stitch, as she was known, leaned into Willie's truck as he asked her to go with him back to his place. At first, Stitch refused, as Coquitlam was too far away, but when Willie offered her $100 for her time and promised to have her back within an hour, she relented and got into the truck.

On the drive to the farm, Stitch noticed a woman's bra on the seat and asked Willie who it belonged to. He brushed it off as belonging to a date he had had the previous week. However, something didn't sit quite right with Stitch and she began to feel uneasy. There was no way to escape from the moving truck, so she had no choice but to continue with her journey.

Willie led Stitch through the trailer. As they passed through the rancid kitchen, she noticed a large butcher's knife on the table, which only added to her unease. As they reached the room at the end, Stitch noticed the room had no bed, just a sleeping bag on the floor and a roll of clear plastic. She asked Willie if she could use his phone to call her boyfriend to let him know where she was.

As she looked for his number, Willie grabbed her hand from behind and secured a pair of handcuffs on her wrist. All Stitch could think about was that butcher's knife in the kitchen, and she knew he was going to kill her, so she fought back with every ounce of her being. A violent struggle ensued, and Stitch managed to stab Willie before escaping the trailer and making her way painfully to the road. A couple who were driving past stopped for her and called an ambulance.

Stitch was in a bad way. She had sustained four stab wounds at the hands of Pickton – two in the abdomen, one on her left arm, and one in the ribs which had punctured her lung. At the same time, Pickton had managed to drive himself to the same hospital with his own injuries which Stitch had managed to inflict.

An orderly at the hospital discovered a key in Willie's pocket which opened the handcuffs on Stitch's wrist, and Willie was arrested and charged with four offences, one of which was attempted murder.

Stitch's lifestyle worked in Willie's favor, however, and the charges were dropped as it was felt that she was an unreliable witness due to her drug use and work as a prostitute.

Willie was a free man.

Missing Women

During 1994 and 1995, the Picktons sold off some of their land to developers. The area was expanding, and their land was valuable, so selling it made the Picktons quite wealthy. But with the wealth came the scroungers.

People whom Willie barely knew suddenly came out of the woodwork looking for handouts – homeless people, drug addicts, and prostitutes, all wanting money, or a place to stay, or a car – and Willie gave it to them. Having been written off as useless all his life, this was probably the first time he felt useful.

By 1997 a pattern was emerging in Downtown Eastside – more than a dozen women had gone missing, but because of the nature of the area, and of the women themselves, their disappearance didn't cause concern.

However, when another woman named Marnie Frey disappeared, her family raised the alarm. Marnie had been a good girl, who had done well at school, but by the time she had reached her 20s she had fallen in with a bad crowd and become addicted to cocaine and heroin. Her family had often brought her home sick from the drugs, but as soon as she was well enough she would leave again to pursue her habit.

One thing Marnie always did, though, was contact her family on her birthday, so when, on August 30th, 1997, she didn't call or come home for her birthday celebrations her family thought it odd, and when over a week had passed with no contact they raised the alarm.

Her family went to the police and asked them to help, to check whether Marnie had collected her social assistance payments, but they didn't receive any answers. The thinking was always the same – she's probably just moved on.

One police officer did take notice, though. A beat cop named Dave Dickson had worked the area for years and had become accustomed to seeing the same people day in and day out. But it gradually dawned on him that some of the area's familiar faces were missing, and he began to make a list of names. When he checked these names against social services records, he discovered that their social assistance payments hadn't been collected and he knew then that something was seriously wrong.

In the meantime, more and more women were disappearing from the streets of Vancouver.[2] On January 7th, 1998, Kerry Lynn Koski, a 38-year-old mother of three went missing, and in February Inga Monique Hall, a German-born mother and grandmother in her 40s was also seen for the last time.[3] But it wasn't until April of that year that another missing woman's friends and family, like the Freys, raised the alarm.

28-year-old Sarah De Vries had a loving adoptive family, and she had also struck up an unlikely friendship with a former punter of hers – Wayne Lang. So when Sarah disappeared, Wayne launched a poster campaign, asking for help from anyone and everyone in the community to find Sarah.

First Lead

At the same time as Wayne Lang was searching for Sarah, Dave Dickson was also working on the case. By June 1998 his list of missing women stood at 31, and he believed he had enough information to take the case to his superior – Staff Sgt Doug Mackay-Dunn. Along with his own observations, Dickson had also asked his wife, a nurse, whether she had noticed any of her 'regulars' had gone missing. She had.

But without bodies or crime scenes, the police's hands were tied and they could not or would not open a murder inquiry. Instead, they assigned an extra officer to missing persons.

Wayne Lang had set up an information hotline for information on Sarah De Vries, but months passed with nothing but crank calls and false sightings. But one day he received a call from a man who identified himself as Bill Hiscox. Bill told Lang that the police needed to investigate a local pig farmer named Willie Pickton. According to Bill, a friend of his worked at the farm and was a friend of Pickton's, and she had told Bill that she had seen some strange things while she was cleaning – items of women's clothing, and women's IDs and that some of the clothing was bloodstained. When she had asked Willie about the items he had told her to get rid of them. According to Bill, the woman, Lisa Yelds, told him that she thought the farm was where the missing women had been taken. Bill told her that she needed to call the police, or that he would do it. She refused, so Bill made the call.

The police, at last, took notice, and they interviewed Lisa Yelds. Lisa denied everything – because she hated cops.

"The reason I didn't say much to the cops…is for one I hate cops. And two, I didn't see anything. You give a cop an inch and they take a mile.

*They turn around, they take the story, twist it ten ways to Sunday and blow it up. So then you're sitting in a pile of s**t which you didn't even say in the first f***ing place and they're twisting it in your face."*

Without Lisa's statement, the police were unable to get a warrant, and without a warrant, any evidence obtained would be inadmissible.

The Investigation

Despite Lisa Yelds' statement, all was not lost. A homicide detective, Ron Lepine, was assigned to the case, and it was his job to draw up a list of possible suspects who might be responsible for the disappearances. Men with a history of violence towards women, in particular towards prostitutes. The list was long. There were dozens who had been convicted of violence towards prostitutes, and many more who had been charged but not convicted. Among the names was Willie Pickton, flagged because of his assault on Stitch two years earlier. But even as the names were being gathered, more women went missing.

By February 1999 there were more comings and goings on the Pickton farm. Scroungers came and went and Willie continued to give handouts to those who asked.

One of the new arrivals was Andy Bellwood, an addict who had just come out of rehab. He was desperate to get back on his feet, and when one of Willie's friends introduced them to each other, Willie offered Andy a place to stay and gave him odd jobs to do around the farm.

Andy was grateful, and he and Willie got on like a house on fire. To Andy, Willie seemed kind, caring and generous, and the pair quickly struck up a close friendship.

But the relationship turned sour after just one month. While Andy was watching TV, Willie came in and sat down on the bed, trying to cajole Andy into picking up a prostitute with him. Andy declined, but Willie kept insisting. When he saw Andy wasn't going to change his mind, Willie reached under the bed and withdrew a leather belt, along with some wire and a pair of handcuffs before kneeling on the bed.

As Andy watched, Willie simulated caressing a woman, before pretending to attach handcuffs to her. He then took the leather belt and simulated putting it around her throat and strangling her with it.

When he sat back down he looked Andy in the eye.

"Do you know how much people bleed? You wouldn't believe how much people bleed. After that, I take them to the barn, hang them, and gut them."

Four days later, Andy was taken to one side by two of Pickton's men and beaten, as they accused him of stealing equipment from Willie – something he denied. He believed it was Willie's way of warning him to keep his mouth shut about what had transpired that night in the bedroom.

Andy had had enough. He took the next ferry to Vancouver Island and didn't look back.

What Andy didn't know was that, with Pickton already flagged on the system, his information could have escalated the investigation and granted them the warrant they so desperately needed to look at Pickton more closely.

Lynn Ellingsen

At around the same time as Andy Bellwood arrived at the farm, another addict did too. Her name was Lynn Ellingsen. Lynn couldn't believe her luck – Willie would set her easy tasks to do around the farm, such as answering the phone, and in return would pay her good money, which she invariably spent on drugs. Her habit spiralled from spending $20 a day to up to $200 a day with the wages that Willie paid her.

According to Andy Bellwood, Ellingsen was present at his beating, an accusation she denied. But even if she was, it didn't put her off hanging around Pickton.

On March 20th, 1999, Willie drove to his usual haunt to pick up a hooker and asked Ellingsen along for company. He stopped at the side of the road and called to the girl standing there, asking her to go back to the farm with him. The girl was reluctant but saw that Ellingsen was there. The girl asked her if she was going too, and when Ellingsen told her she was staying at the farm the girl agreed to go.

Back at the farm, Willie took her to his room, and Ellingsen went to hers, but something made her come back out and walk along the corridor to Willie's. His room was empty. Ellingsen went to the window and looked out. The light was on in the barn where Willie slaughtered his pigs, so Ellingsen went outside to see what was going on.

As the barn door closed behind her, Lynn Ellingsen saw the girl she and Willie had picked up earlier that evening, hanging from the ceiling.[4]

"He was cutting something...there was blood everywhere. I just remember staring at her feet."

Lynn elaborated on her story, saying that the woman was hanging from a chain and that there was long black hair on the table.

"[she was hanging] the same way he hung his pigs. There was a chain right there. That's where she was, where he does his pigs."[5]

Pickton pulled Ellingsen to one side and warned her that if she ever told anyone, she would be hanging next to the girl. It was enough to scare Ellingsen – that and the opportunity to glean more money from him in return for her silence.

In the first part of 1999 women continued to disappear, and the police had over 100 suspects in their sights. At last the case had attracted public attention, as well as interest from the media. The missing women were even featured on an episode of America's Most Wanted in July 1999, but still, the police had no bodies, and no crime scene – in effect they had no crimes.

But that summer they had a breakthrough. A man named Ross Caldwell told police that Lynn Ellingsen had seen a woman being butchered at the Pickton farm. Detective Ron Lepine believed Caldwell and brought him in for an interview, but he didn't make a good witness. Caldwell was high on drugs on the day of the interview, and he was dismissed as being an unreliable witness. Once again, the police found themselves needing an eye witness, so they brought Lynn Ellingsen in for questioning.

Like Lisa Yelds, Ellingsen denied everything. It wasn't until after the interview that Detective Frank Henley realized that she had said something significant. He had been telling her that he didn't believe she would allow another woman to suffer the way the missing women had probably suffered and described a dead body to her. She had replied:

"That's gross. It's yellow and it's gross."

Henley knew that unless Ellingsen had seen a dead body, a cut up body, she wouldn't have known that the fat was yellow.

Henley managed to persuade Ellingsen to agree to a polygraph test, but the day before she was due to undergo the test she disappeared.

Lynn Ellingsen had good reason to protect Willie Pickton. She was using the knowledge she had about him to blackmail him, and she didn't want to wave goodbye to her meal ticket.

Willie Pickton

In late 1999 police had Willie Pickton under surveillance. But they faced a quandary – if he was spotted picking up a prostitute they would have to intervene and show their hand because they couldn't risk another victim. But their subject did nothing of note and their surveillance continued until he was seen with a female in his car. Because of the potential risk to a woman's life, the police had no choice but to stop him. His passenger turned out to be his friend Gina's 13-year-old daughter. Their cover was blown and the investigation stalled.

But on January 19th, 2000 a surprising turn of events came about. Willie Pickton himself turned up at the police station with Gina Houston in tow. Gina and Willie had been friends for a long time, and Willie adored her. They had often talked about getting married, and according to Gina, he wanted the whole deal – marriage, children, and the white picket fence. However, when Willie had presented Gina with a ring years earlier she had rejected him.

The interview with Pickton lasted around six and a half hours, during which he invited the police to look around the farm themselves, claiming that all he wanted to do was clear his name and put an end to the whole thing. Later that same week officers did visit the farm but could find no evidence of anything untoward.

Once again, the police had hit a brick wall.

Joint Task Force

Something had to be done, and it was decided that the Vancouver police and the Royal Canadian Mounted Police would join forces and look at all of the evidence again. But while Project Evenhanded, as it was called, went on, more women disappeared.

Frank Henley couldn't let go of the case, especially after he failed to get Lynn Ellingsen to take the polygraph, so he visited Willie Pickton 'for a chat'.

As Pickton lamented the fact that the police had him under suspicion, Henley casually suggested that he undergo a lie detector test, to which he half-heartedly agreed. Henley had heard the same response before and knew Pickton wouldn't take the test.

When the two men shook hands at the end of the meeting, Henley was repulsed by Pickton's 'gross, wet handshake'. He knew that Willie Pickton fitted the profile perfectly.

In June 2001 a pharmacist reported one of his patients missing. 22-year-old Andrea Joesbury hadn't turned up for her methadone for several days in a row, causing her pharmacist to be concerned for her welfare.

A month later Sereena Abotsway also disappeared. Sereena was a local character who was well known and was missed immediately. Gina Houston, Willie's friend, had seen Sereena at the Pickton farm doing drugs.

Two more women followed – 34-year-old Diane Rock and 26-year-old Mona Wilson.

That fall, Gina Houston went to the farm to collect a pig which Willie had butchered for her, but she noticed something was different. In the barn was a large freezer, and for the first time, the freezer was covered with a blanket. Not only that but it had an array of new tools laid out neatly on the top. As Gina went towards the freezer she noticed Willie standing close by, and when she looked at him he shook his head at her as if to tell her not to open it.

She didn't.

The Breakthrough

By early 2002 Willie Pickton was in the top 40 of suspects being looked at for the missing women. And ex-employee of Pickton's farm, Scott Chubbs, told police that he had seen illegal firearms on the farm. His information wasn't in relation to the missing women, but it gave police the chance they had been waiting for – they were able to gain entry to the farm and begin a search.

They found women's IDs, clothing, syringes, and crucially an asthma inhaler with Sereena Abotsway's name on it. This discovery then gave the police the grounds for a complete search of the property.

Sereena's head, hands and feet were found in a bucket in a freezer, along with the remains of Andrea Joesbury. Bones and teeth belonging to Mona Wilson, Brenda Wolfe, Georgina Papin (thought to be the girl Lynn Ellingsen had seen hanging in the barn), and Marnie Frey.

On February 22nd, 2002, 52-year-old Robert William Pickton was charged with two counts of first-degree murder, with a further four charges following shortly afterwards.[6]

He was eventually charged with 26 counts of murder.

While he was being held in jail, Pickton shared a cell with an undercover police officer. Pickton, believing his cell mate to be genuine, told him that he had murdered 49 and was annoyed because he had wanted to make it a 'round 50', but had gotten sloppy and been caught.

In the meantime, the investigation was the biggest in Canada's history. 200,000 DNA samples were collected, along with 600,000 exhibits from the crime scene. Over 380,000 cubic yards of soil were sifted through in the search for human remains, and the investigation cost in the region of $70 million.

Although Pickton was arrested in 2002 his trial did not begin until 22nd January 2007, due to the sheer size of the case.

The Verdict

On 9th December 2007, Robert William Pickton was found guilty on six counts of second-degree murder – verdicts which shocked the nation. The charges of first-degree murder were dropped because it couldn't be determined whether Pickton had planned the murders. He was sentenced to life imprisonment with no chance of parole for 25 years.

The charges relating to the other 20 women were to be heard in a separate hearing, but these charges were never brought because Pickton had already been given the maximum sentence and further convictions would add nothing to his sentence.

Pickton was never charged with the other 23 murders he claimed to have committed because their identities could not be determined from DNA found, only that of the 26 women he was charged with.[7]

It is not really known what Pickton did to, and with, the bodies of his victims. He told Andy Bellwood that he would feed the bodies to his pigs, and any remains that weren't consumed would be put in barrels and taken to a rendering plant for disposal.[8]

Stories circulated that Pickton ground up some of his victims' flesh and mixed it with pork, selling it to his neighbors.[9] While that has never been proved or disproved, a health official could not rule out the possibility of cross contamination at the farm. When he was further questioned about whether that meant human flesh had found its way into animal meat bound for human consumption, he replied:

"It's very disturbing to think about, but [there is] the possibility of some cross-contamination. But the degree of it or when or how much we really don't know…I think if we could rule it out, we definitely would like to."[10]

What is known is that an official alert was issued to the public asking anyone who had purchased meat from Pickton's farm to contact Vancouver police.[11]

Only six families of Pickton's victims were given closure with the convictions. The other 20 women's families and loved ones weren't given that chance, and while his sentence would not have been lengthened by further convictions, at least those left behind might have had some kind of an end to their nightmare and be able to draw a line under it.

For the families of the other 23 women Pickton claimed to have butchered, their life sentence goes on, never knowing what happened to their daughters, or sisters, or mothers, and that is a sentence which will never have the chance of parole.